In Defense of the Religion of Peace

By

Askari Abdul-Muntaqim

BROKEN LEGACY PUBLISHING SERVICES

Book formatted and Cover layout by **Egeria Consulting**
www.egeriaconsulting.net

CONTENTS

INTRODUCTION

There has been a concerted effort, on the part of those people whose agenda is to defame Islam, to link, inextricably, those who have come to be known as "Islamic Terrorists, " with the religion, of Islam itself. There has been little effort exerted, in an attempt, to treat the religion, of Islam fairly. It is assumed, as a matter of course, that Islam invites to the kind of murderous outrages that humanity has recently witnessed, on the part, of some who claim that Islam is their faith.

The Muslims have an obligation to stand for Islam. We have no right, need or desire, to stand with or for people who seek to destroy Islam through irresponsible speech or conduct, whether from within the religion, or without. In fact, the obligation of the Muslim, is to stand firmly against that which leads to Allah's religion either being defamed or harmed. One is left dumbfounded when we consider that the world's population, of Muslims is in excess, of one billion people, and that of those billion plus people an almost infinitesimal amount of them have embraced murder and indiscriminate war as a "lawful" exercise of jihad, yet Islam's detractors spare no breath, ink, nor effort, in seeking to convince all who have ears, that Islam is inherently violent.

We cannot find people who are asking the question, that if Islam is truly a violent religion which invites to terror and destruction, then why has not it's predominate majority risen up and answered the call to kill man, woman and child, wherever they may be found? Rather, we are, witness to people without integrity, character, or honor, doing all they can to advance and agenda of hate for whatever reason. They use every opportunity to make claims against Islam, which cannot, in truth, survive the scrutiny of objective analysis.

If a real interest exists, in understanding what has quite unfairly been dubbed "Islamic terrorism," there is, perhaps, some wisdom in seeking to understand what it is not. The claims have been made and firmly established, in the minds of most, that so-called Islamic terrorism is a manifestation of the Islamic faith. It has been said that the Qur'an gives license to Terrorists, and encourages their murderous conduct. This is either true or not, and since the Qur'an is not an obscure, esoteric and inaccessible text, we can examine the Qur'an to determine if there is any truth to those claims.

As has been said before understanding what so-called Islamic Terrorism is not, is fundamentally necessary to beginning the process, of understanding what it is. This work does not seek to explain or expound upon what is "Islamic Terrorism", but rather defend the religion, of Islam, against the defamatory claims that Islam invites, in any way, to targeting civilian populations of non-combatant people, of any faith and that Islam calls for unrestricted warfare against people who don't share the belief, of the Muslims.

In an effort to demonstrate what cannot be properly called Islamic Terrorism, there needs to be an effort to show what Islam says about the activities, of those who have come to be known as Islamic Terrorists. To do this, it is necessary to peer, for a moment, into the Islamic mind. The Islamic mind is informed, guided and motivated primarily, by the Qur'an, and then by he who was the living example, of the Qur'an. We are required to give deference to the life and conduct, of the Prophet of Islam Muhammad ibn Abdullah (SAW). Once a commandment or prohibition has been confirmed to have derived from one of these two sources, the Muslim, is not permitted to challenge these commandments or prohibitions. Human logic or reason cannot be introduced, seeking to abrogate or abridge these established texts. The Muslims hold that the Qur'an and the Prophet Muhammad's (SAW) guidance is sacred and inviolable. When a Muslim is found not to hold this belief, he has deviated, from the faith, and one can no longer hold that his actions are the product, of the Islamic mind.

The proof of this statement, can be found, in the Qur'an, when we look to the Qur'an we find what it means:

> "It is not for a believing man or a believing woman when Allah and His Messenger have decided a matter that they should (thereafter) have any choice about their affair. And Whoever disobeys Allah and His Messenger has certainly fallen to error"
>
> (Qur'an 33:36)

It can, therefore, be seen that the two sources of law, and tradition, in Islam, are the Qur'an and the Sunnah, the Sunnah is properly understood as the Prophet Muhammad's (SAW) guidance, to the Muslims. And it should be understood that where the Muslim finds a verse, in the Qur'an, or it reaches him that the Prophet Muhammad's (Saw) guidance, is a thing certain, then they "Should (thereafter) have (no) choice about their affair." Such stringent requirements, of the acceptance, for behavior and belief, make it possible to immediately juxtapose conduct on the part, of the Muslim, and then determine whether or not it can be considered to be proper Islamic behavior.

The aforementioned verse makes it clear, to the Muslim that where there is a commandment or prohibition found, in the Qur'an, or the Sunnah that the Muslim is powerless except to enact he commandment or abstain from the prohibited matter. Where the verse says what means: "When Allah and His Messenger," this refers to the Qur'an (Allah's speech) and the Sunnah of the Prophet Muhammad (SAW).

The question that arises is a simple one, are these people who have quite incorrectly been labeled and have come to be known as "Islamic fundamentalist" truly following the Qur'an and the Sunnah, are they, in truth, acting in accordance with the fundamentals of the religion of Islam. If an objective look at the textual evidence determines that these terrorist, murdering thugs are in fact, following the Qur'an and the Sunnah, then it will be established that Islam is not a religion of peace, and as such Islam has no valid claim to righteousness. Correspondingly if we find that Islam prohibits these acts of terror and crimes against humanity, and it is further found that Islam invites to the direct opposite, than all objective readers will have to conclude that Islam is, indeed a religion of peace. That too would necessitate that those acting, in its name whose behavior is antithetical to the establishment or restoration of peace, are not acting according to, the fundamentals, of the religion, of Islam.

This work seeks as its objective, Insha'Allah, to bring clarity to these issues and to answer, definitively, the question of whether or not the religion of Islam is, in truth, a religion of peace.

May Allah (SWT) allow Muslims and non-Muslims alike to come to a greater understanding of the religion of Islam. The Religion of Peace. **Ameen**

Chapter 1

PROOF AGAINST WHAT THEY CLAIM

There are far more pressing issues before humanity than what has unfairly been dubbed "Islamic Terrorism", but these crimes against humanity rank right up there with the other problems that threaten the stability of the world. World stability has throughout the ages have faced threats, and humanity has, with varying degrees of success, always sought to maintain stability if, in the eyes of modern man, this stability has been achieved in the most perverse of manners.

People the world over have through whatever mechanisms, developed judgments on certain behaviors,and as such there is no universally accepted code of conduct. What is fair to some is barbaric to others. One need not look further than the debate that is ever raging over the destruction of human fetuses in the United States and other places around the world. One would think that if there could exist a single issue on which there could be universal consensus, that it would be, on the issue of whether or not it is morally acceptable to end the life of an unborn child. One would think that a basic universally accepted truth is that it is morally repugnant to murder children, unborn or otherwise, but the perfect reality is that moral universality does not exist.

1

Given the absence of a universal human code of moral conduct, any given people have to develop, inherit and or utilize some means by which to judge behavior. With all these varying and subjective components in use, judgments will defer from one people to another, even from one person to the next. So, I don't believe that we should find it strange that what most of humanity calls terror, some call legitimate resistance. After all, these are judgments born of definitions that change depending on who is carrying out the acts. For example when the military of a country targets an entire apartment complex, in an effort, to assassinate one terrorist leader, this is considered a legitimate police action. On the other hand, if a group of self-proclaimed resistance fighters parked a truck bomb, next to the apartment building, targeting a single government official who had previously ordered an apartment building be bombed with all its inhabitants present, that act would no doubt be considered an act of terror.

People will argue, without resolution, as to if either or both acts are acts of terror, each coming to very different conclusions depending upon there sensibilities. This is because the conclusions are based on criterion which is accepted or rejected based on one's sensibilities. The only real way to come to agreement on such issues is to apply, across the board, a universal standard which applies to both friend and foe. It can be said, for example, that

2

deliberately targeting civilian population for killing or mass casualties, seeking to achieve a political or military objective is either acceptable conduct or it is not. It is both unfair and self-defeating to call it terror when the conduct is directed at you or those friendly to you, but seek to justify the same act when it is directed against those whom you oppose.

One would be fool-hearted, in deed, to assert that there does not exist a crisis within the ranks of the Muslims, as it relates to some Muslims adopting terror as an Islamic tactic. The most important question arising from this circumstance is one of legality. We find that many people who have adopted animus toward Islam, claim that, Islamically speaking, terror is sanctioned as a matter of religion. It goes without saying that the practitioners of terror tactics hold this to be a lawful, accepted and wholly legitimate practice not only sanctioned by the religion, but commanded by Allah. The claims, of both, of these groups, must be tested.

While it is understandable that the non-Muslim will be ignorant of the intricacies of the Islamic faith, it is somewhat disturbing to note that must Muslims themselves possess this same level of ignorance. It is due to this ignorance that many Muslims and non-Muslims alike examine verses in the Qur'an and conclude, without further investigation, that the verse being read represents a definitive ruling. While it may be true that in some cases verses from the Qur'an can be viewed and the full impact and import of the verse can be known without further examination of additional verses and or other explanatory sources, it is not an accepted method of understanding the Qur'an.

The MUFASIREEN, or the scholars dedicated to the Science of Qur'an explanation, reject interpretation of Qur'an based on mere opinion. Equally rejected is the ability of the reader to approach the text without knowledge of the sciences of (understanding) the Qur'an and derive therefrom legal rulings. Therefore, when we find Muslims and or non-Muslims going to the Qur'an, reading various verses and then claiming that, on the basis of this reading, they can definitively conclude Islam commands this or prohibits that we simply reject this. It should be known that this is also rejected, by the people of knowledge. This, of course, has not prevented people from engaging in this practice.

Throughout the Qur'an one can find what may be called "Martial Verses". These are verses that invite to combat, killing, ambush, and harsh treatment of various groups of people. Enemies of Islam, if they call themselves Muslim or otherwise, have seized upon these verses to advance their private agendas. In some cases these verses have been used to justify the wanton and indiscriminate murder of men, women and children the world over, and others use these verses seeking to demonstrate that

Islam is an ungodly, if not demonic grouping of archaic traditions, devoid of human decency or useful spiritual guidance.

Ahmad Von Denffer, in a work which is of great benefit to all who seek to understand the position of the Qur'an, in the lives of the Muslims, wrote in a text which the entitled <u>Ulum al-Quran the introduction to the sciences of the Qur'an</u>, : Tafsir (exegesis) of the Qur'an is the most important science for Muslims. All matters concerning the Islamic way of life are connected to it in one sense or another, since the right application of Islam is based on proper understanding of the guidance from Allah. Without tafsir there would be no right understanding of various passages of the Qur'an."

When we look to the book of Allah, we find the 21st verse of chapter 33 which says:

> There has certainly been for you in the Messenger of Allah an excellent example for anyone whose hope is in Allah and the Last Day, and (who) remember Allah often. (Qur'an 33:21)

We therefore conclude that when seeking to understand the Qur'an the example has to be that of Messenger of Allah. So we should seek to know how it is that he understood a particular verse, and what we can understand of the practical examples that he (saw) left to us concerning them. Further, it follows that if we understand a verse in a way that is contrary to the understanding of the Messenger of Allah, we are then obligated to leave off our own understanding and apply that of Allah's Messenger.

Returning to Qur'an we find verses that speak very directly to fighting the enemies of Islam. These verses, as we have explained earlier, have been seized upon by the enemies of Islam, both, from within and without, to either approve acts of terror or to prove that Islam invites to these acts. An understanding, of the circumstances surrounding their revelation, will be extremely helpful in understanding their true import and impact. It will also permit us to make a definitive determination as to the ability, of the reader, to take these verses as proofs, wherewith he can argue, for the position that the Qur'an both allows and invites to the wanton destruction of property and complete disregard for the lives of others.

It is important to note that those who use verses of the Qur'an for nefarious purposed, not only take verses out of context, but also ignore other verses which serve to explain the very verses they seek to distort. Additionally, in some cases they only take a portion of a verse, which agrees with their premise and ignore the portion of the verse that destroys it. One example of this may be found when we look to the use of Surah (chapter) 2 Ayaat (verses) 191-193. Distortionists are fond of the verses, but you will note that they will not cite these verses in their entirety. You will hear them say, "The Qur'an says what follows:

> "And kill them wherever you find them...such is the recompense for the disbelievers..."

> "fight them until there is no more oppression and religion is made for Allah Alone."

This, in the minds of some, gives justification for unrestricted warfare on people belonging to a nation who is either actively or passively engaged in fighting against the Muslims anywhere in the world. For these verses are used to attack Islam as a religion of intolerance and hate. If read, as they have been presented above, these verses may well form the rudiments for such an argument, but when we view the verses in their entirety, we find a context that gives lie to such claims. Taken together, they say what means:

> "Fight in the way of Allah those who fight you but do not transgress. Indeed, Allah does not like transgressors"

> "And kill them wherever you overtake them and expel them from wherever they have expelled you, and oppression is worse than killing. And do not fight them at Masjid Al-Haram unless they fight you there.

But if they fight you kill them. That is the recompense of the disbeliever."

"And if they cease, then, indeed, Allah is Forgiving, Merciful."

"Fight them until there is no (more) oppression and religion is made for Allah Alone. But if they cease, there is no aggression except against the oppressor."

One can very easily see that when viewed in their entirety, and the addition of verse 190 is allowed to proceed them, these verses lack the impact necessary to make good sound bites, for those who seek to use them as proofs for unrestricted warfare. These verses are further elucidated when the context, in which they were revealed is known.

The Prophet Muhammad (saw) was born to the people of Quraysh who were the premiere tribe of Arabia, but more importantly they occupied, chiefly the city of Makka where in is "Masjid Al-Haram". When the Prophet (saw0 came, to his people, with the message that there is no God except Allah (God), they rejected this message and after the passage of time constructively evicted the Prophet (saw) and his followers from not only Masjid al-Haram, but their homes as well. This was accomplished through "Fitnah" (i.e. oppression, torture, murder, and disenfranchisement.) Life became unbearable and they migrated, to the city of Madinah.

Verse 2:190-193 speaks to those events and one that had not yet occurred. Here Allah was telling the believers that those people who had engaged, in oppression, killing, and fighting against the Muslims, must be fought, in kind. Not only that, but that they must be expelled from Masjid al-Haram eventually, however they were not to be attack there unless they, the disbelievers, initiated hostilities. We note that Masjid al-Haram was then and remains still this day, the first most sacred site in Islam.

Verse 2:190 when read and understood correctly directs the Muslim forces to engage the "combative forces" of the disbelieving people of Makka, "Fight, in the cause of Allah, those who fight you, but do not transgress..."Allah admonishes the Muslims forces that fighting people who have not "fought them" is a transgression. Allah (swt) further admonishes the Muslims that He (swt) does not like the transgressor. Claims that the above verses of Al-Quran can be used as a justification for targeting not combatants, in an unrestricted war, cannot stand. While other verses, which we shall examine, Insha'Allah, make clear that giving aid and support to a combative force is considered an act of war for which one can be fought.

We will exam a number of verses, in the Qur'an, in like fashion. Our examination will, Insha'Allah, allow us to give critical thought to the real meaning, of these verses and clarify what Islam says about Jihad (The Islamic struggle against evil both within oneself and without).

There is a prevalent notion, in the minds of radical Muslims and, by extension, in the minds or those who get there understanding of Islam from the conduct and rhetoric of radical Muslims, that both the Qur'an and Islam invite hatred of Christians and Jews. Nothing could be further from the truth, but the fact remains that there are verses, in the Qur'an that speak to the necessity and permissibility of not only treating Christians and Jews with harshness, but to also fight against them. These verses, like all verses in any revealed Holy Book, have a context and cannot be understood or applied without first finding and then understanding the context in which they were revealed. For example we find what means:

> "And He brought down those who supported them among the people of the scripture from their fortresses and cast terror into their hearts [so that] a party [i.e. their men] you killed and you took a party captive [i.e. the women and children]"

10

"And He caused you to inherit their land and their homes and their properties and a land which you have not trodden and ever is Allah, over all things, Competent." Qur'an 33:26-27

Many point to these verses and claim that Christians and Jews are to be targeted and killed. A fair reading will show this to be false, but perhaps some explanation is necessary. The Prophet Muhammad (saw) was forced to defend the city of Madinah from an organized and consorted attack by a number of Arabs tribes. When the Prophet (saw) had first migrated to Madinah, he (saw) entered into a non-aggression pact, with all the tribes of the city, the Jewish tribes included. The above two verses deal with a Jewish tribe that had agreed not to aid and support anybody against the Muslims in war. They broke that agreement and were fought. The final result of the engagement was the execution of all the men, and the taking captive of the women and children. The verse does not give license, for all time, for the Muslims to fight the Jews (or Christians), to kill their men and then take captive their women and children. These verses recount a historical event and gives guidance as to how, in the future, to deal with any people who behave in a like manner. This is not a blanket indictment, of the Jews and or the Christians. Whoever takes these verses to have this meaning has failed to understand them correctly and have ignored all that is necessary to properly approach the Qur'an.

In chapter two the reader will have the opportunity to assess first-hand the dangers of taking text and making assertion about select verses, without seeking to understand context. What follows here are many of the verses which cause much controversy regarding the matter currently under discussion.

> "Fighting has been enjoined upon you while it is hateful to you. But perhaps you hate a thing and it is good for you; and perhaps you love a thing and it is bad for you. And Allah knows, while you know not." Qur'an2:1216

> "You are the best nation produced (as an example) for mankind. You enjoin what is right and forbid what it wrong and believe in Allah. If only the people of the scripture had believed, it would have been better for them. Among them are believers, but most of them are defiantly disobedient."

> "They have been put under humiliation (by Allah) wherever they are overtaken, except for a rope (i.e. covenant) from Allah and a rope (i.e. treaty) from the people (i.e. the Muslims). And they have drawn upon

themselves anger from Allah and have been put under destitution. That is because they disbelieved in (i.e. rejected) the verses of Allah and killed the Prophets without right. That is because they disobeyed and (habitually) transgressed." Qur'an 3:110 & 112

"And if you are killed, in the cause of Allah or die – then forgiveness from Allah and mercy are better than whatever they accumulate (in this world)

"And whether you die or are killed, unto Allah you will be gathered." Qur'an 3:157-158

"Those who believe fight in the cause of Allah, disbelievers fight, in the cause of Taghut. So Fight against the allies of Satan. Indeed, the plot of Satan, has ever been weak." Qur'an 4:75

"They wish you would disbelieve as they disbelieved, so you would be alike. So do not take from among them allies until they emigrate for the case of Allah,. But if they turn away (i.e. refuse) then seize them and kill them wherever you find them and take not from among then any ally or helper." Qur'an 4:89

"O you who believe, do not take Jews and Christians as allies. They are (in fact) allies of one another. And whoever is an ally to them among you – then indeed, he is (one) of them. Indeed, Allah guides not the wrong doing people." Qur'an 5:51

"Say 'shall I inform you of (what is) worse than that as penalty from Allah? (it is that of) those whom Allah has cursed and with whom He became angry and made of them Apes and pigs and slaves of Taghut. (false gods, corrupt entities). Those are worse, in position and further astray from the sound way." Qur'an 5:60

"And let not those who disbelieve think they will escape. Indeed, they will not cause failure to Allah."

"And prepare against them whatever you are able of power and of steeds of war by which you may terrify the enemy of Allah and your enemy and others besides them whom you do not know (but) whom Allah knows. And whatever you spend, in the cause of Allah will be fully repaid to you, and you will not be wronged." Qur'an 8:59-60

"It is not for a Prophet to have captives (of war) until he inflicts a massacre (upon Allah's enemies) in the land. You (i.e. some Muslims) desires the commodities of this world, but Allah desires (for you) the hereafter And Allah is Exalted, in Might, and Wise." Qur'an 8:67

"Indeed Allah has purchased, from the believers, their lives and their properties (in exchange) for that they will have paradise. They fight, in the cause of Allah, so they kill and are killed. (It is) a true promise (binding) upon Him, in the Torah and The gospel and the Qur'an. And who is truer to his covenant than Allah? So rejoice, in your transaction which you have contracted. And it is that which is the great attainment." Qur'an 9:111

"And when the sacred months have passed, then kill the polytheist wherever you find them at every place of ambush But if they should repent, establish prayer and gives Zakah, (a tax due to the poor from the rich) let them (go) on their way, Indeed, Allah is Forgiving and Merciful." Qur'an 9:12

"Fight them, Allah will punish them by your hands and will disgrace them and give you victory over them and satisfy the breast (i.e. desires) of a believing people." Qur'an 9:14

"Fight those who do not believe in Allah or in the Last day and who do not consider unlawful what Allah and

His Messenger have made unlawful and the religion of truth (i.e. Islam) from those who were given the scripture (i.e. Christians and Jews) (Fight them) until they give the Jizyah willingly, while they are humbled. Qur'an 9:29

"And if you punish (an enemy, o believers), punish with an equivalent of that with which you were harmed. But if you are patient it is better for those who are patient." Qur'an 16:126

"Permission (to fight) has been given to those who are being fought, because they were wronged. And Indeed, Allah is competent to give them victory." Qur'an 22:39

"And when you meet those who disbelieve (in battle) strike (their) necks until, when you have afflicted slaughter upon them, then secure their bonds, and either (confer) favor afterward or ransom (them) until the war lays down its burdens. That (is the command). And if Allah willed. He could have taken vengeance upon them (Himself), but (He ordered armed struggle) to test some of you by means of others. And those who are killed in the cause of Allah – never will He waste their deeds." Qur'an 47:4

"Muhammad is the Messenger of Allah, and those with him are forceful against the disbelievers, merciful among themselves. You see them bowing and prostrating (in prayer), seeking bounty from Allah and (His) pleasure..." Qur'an 48:29

"O you who have believed, do not take my enemies and your enemies as allies extending to them affection while they have disbelieved in what came to you of the truth, having driven out the Prophet and yourselves (only) because you believe in Allah, your Lord. If you have come out for Jihad (i.e. fighting, striving) in my cause and seeking means to my approval, (take them not as friends)..." Qur'an 60:1

These, of course, are not all of the verses in which fighting is mentioned. They, however, do represent those verses that are used by enemies of Islam to cast disparaging aversions on the religion. We have stated earlier that taking any text, but this text in particular (i.e. The Qur'an), out of context results in a distortion of the meaning of the text itself, to say nothing of the verses being quoted. The Muslims maintain that Islam is a religion of peace. They maintain that aggression, in the form of oppressive conduct, is never, under any circumstance, permitted. The Muslims make clear that it is their belief that the taking of innocent life is a crime, moreover a sin for which the perpetrator will be punished possibly in this life, but most certainly in the next.

The single most effective way to debunk these claims would be to produce verses from the Qur'an that belie them. Certainly some of the verses presented above appear to do that. The perfect reality is that not one of these verses can be used to justify the mistreatment of a single human being, be he or she Muslim, Jew, Christian, Buddhist, Hindu or otherwise. Yes, one can take some of these verses in isolation, devoid of context and make them mean whatever he or she desires them to mean, but can these distortions live, in the light of scrutiny? No, they cannot!

It is perhaps instructive to remind the reader that Islam holds that the only true measure of validity, for any action, is what we find, in the Qur'an and what was sent to Allah's Messenger Muhammad ibn Abdullah (saw) left to us by way of what we have said is his (saw) Sunnah.

This text is not the proper place to bring forth all of the arguments that exist against those who claim to be Muslims, yet do not rule by the Book of Allah (i.e. Qur'an) or the Sunnah of His Prophet (saw). It, however, needs to be mentioned that there are various groups of people who call themselves Muslims who do not use the Qur'an and the Sunnah as a guide as to what is right and what is wrong. Many of these people invented and innovated methods for such determinations, all of which are rejected by Islam.

We cannot and do not seek to expound, upon all of the beliefs held by those deviant groups claiming to be Muslims, we instead put forth the proposition what the only true Islam, is Islam, as practiced by the Prophet Muhammad (saw) and those who follow strictly what he (saw) commanded and or prohibited. The reader must, as he will, decide if he believes that proposition to be valid. That notwithstanding, there is universal agreement that the Qur'an is the book on which Muslims claim to base their religion. As such the Qur'an is the best barometer as to what is and is not Islamically acceptable, as well as what is and is not fundamentally a part of the religion.

There can be no better way to understand the Qur'an, its import, or impact, its commandments, its prohibitions, than to understand these through the Qur'an itself. When seeking to know the true meaning of a verse, it is important to look to other verses, in the Qur'an, that address the subject. In so doing, one gains a clear and comprehensive view of the meaning of the entire text and not just the verse being read.

The Qur'an, as it can be assumed, of all text, has an overarching theme. In the Qur'an, the overarching theme is that mankind was placed, on the planet, to worship Allah (God) and Allah alone, and that each human being has a responsibility to fulfill this purpose. There is a no more central theme in the Qur'an and, in truth, everything else found in the book is there only for the purpose of facilitating the fulfillment of this obligation. Whether or not a verse speaks of marriage, divorce, peace treaties, or declarations of war, whether they speak to charity, or migration, all of them do so, in a context, of providing guidance designed to make easy the way for mankind to approach and correctly worship Allah.

It stands to reason that if Allah sent a book (i.e. the Qur'an) as guidance to mankind to explain man's obligation to worship Allah, in the manner that He (swt) Himself desires to be worshiped, that inherent in His (swt) sending of the book was the need for mankind to have free and unfettered access to not only the book itself, but the opportunity, if one so chooses, to act, on the guidance, found in the book. Logic would dictate that should there be any obstacles to accessing this opportunity, that those who believe that Allah had, indeed, sent this book and sent it for this purpose, would have a divine obligation to do what they could to remove those obstacles and impediments. This is the belief, of the Muslims.

When it is understood that the Muslim views the Qur'an as a book of guidance indeed guidance to the correct worship of Allah, it can be understood that no verse in the Qur'an can be interrupted in a way that defeats the purpose of the book; that being to invite mankind, to the worship of Allah and Allah alone.

What is equally true is that every verse in the Qur'an must be understood in the context of the purpose of the book, again inviting mankind to the worship of Allah and Allah alone. So it can be said that all of the "Martial Verses", that is those verses which invite to fighting, killing, ambush, and the harsh treatment of various peoples, have to be understood in the context of inviting mankind to worshiping Allah (swt) and Allah alone.

There may be some difficulty in understanding how this could be. How could it be that fighting and killing, that destruction of life and property are legitimate means by which to invite mankind to the worship of God? Perhaps there is some difficulty, in understanding this, but not so much when fighting, killing, the destruction of life and property is placed in its proper context. In light of that we should perhaps examine the verses to see whether or not they're consistent with righteousness or terror.

We begin with once again viewing Surah 2: verses 190-193:

> "Fight, in the way of Allah, those who fight you, but do not transgress. Indeed Allah does not like the transgressor." 2:190

What is important in this verse is that there is a clear commandment to fight against those who are fighting against the Muslims. Every nation, every people have a right to self-defense. Here Allah is making clear to the Muslims that they have not only a right to defend themselves, but a religious obligation to do so.

> "And those who, when, tyranny strikes them, they defended themselves." 42:39

The other matter of importance found, in the verse, is the commandment not to exceed what is just, in the fight. And then we see Allah's denunciation, of the transgressors.

> "And kill them wherever you overtake them and expel them from wherever they have expelled you, and fitnah is worse than killing. And do not fight them at Masjid-ul-Haram until they fight you there. But if they fight you, then kill them. Such is the recompense of the disbelievers. Qur'an 2:191

> "and if they cease, then, indeed, Allah is forgiving, Merciful." 2:192

> "Fight them until there is no (more) Fitnah and religion is made for Allah alone. But if they cease, there is no aggression except against the oppressor." 2:193

Here we find verses that speak to defense of one's self against hostile acts. Yes, there is no question that Islam teaches that when you meet the enemy on the field of battle that the objective is to kill him dead. However, if the enemy inclines toward peace, then the Muslims are to disengage with him and continue to fight only those who are engaged in fighting the faithful (i.e. Muslims). I am not certain how the verses can be understood any other way, and if they are understood correctly they cannot be said to be verses which call to hatred or oppression of anyone. The fight continues only so long as the enemies of Islam bar people through "Fitnah" from the opportunity to worship Allah Alone. When the "Fitnah" stops, so does the Muslims war effort.

> "Fighting has been enjoined upon you while it is hateful to you, but perhaps you hate a thing and it is good for you; and perhaps you love a thing and it is bad for you. And Allah knows while you know not."
> 2:116

The Muslim is reminded of this obligation to fight, in the cause of Allah, when fighting is necessary, even though fighting involves those things which are hated. For example: killing, dying, being maimed, or taken captive and the expenditure of wealth. On the other side there is a love of peaceful existence, life, health, freedom and keeping one's wealth. These things, the Muslim is admonished, may be harmful to his soul if he allows them to prevent him from doing his duty to defend the faith. The verses before and behind 2:116 make clear that Allah is prompting the believers to appreciate the reason that fighting for the faith is necessary.

The following three verses have often been used to support the argument that the Qur'an invites to the distrust and disdain of the People of the Book (Christians and Jews). Such people argue that when the treatment of Christians and Jews is dealt with and examined, in the Qur'an, one can only find a preponderance of evidence that suggest that the People of the book are not only to be distrusted but despised as well. We will look at the verses and then, Insha'Allah, continue our discussion on the other side.

> "You (i.e. Muslims) are the best nation produced (as an example) for mankind. You enjoin what is right and forbid what is wrong and believe in Allah. If only the people of the scripture had believed, it would have been better for them. Among them are believers, but most of them are defiantly disobedient.

> "They will not harm you except for (some) annoyance. And if they fight you, they will show you their backs (i.e. retreat), then they will not be aided.

"they have been put under humiliation (by Allah) wherever they are overtaken, except for a rope (i.e. covenant) from Allah and rope (i.e. treaty) from the people (i.e. Muslims). And they have drawn upon themselves anger from Allah and have been put under destitution. That is because they disbelieved in (i.e. rejected) the verses of Allah and killed the Prophets without right. That is because they disobey and (habitually) transgressed." 3:110-112

Here these three verses, while addressed to the "People o the scripture", a definition used in other places in the Qur'an to refer to Jews as well as Christians, the reference here is directed exclusively as the Jews. This can be known due to this reason: The later part of verse 112 speaks about a people who killed prophets, in defiance to right. The Qur'an makes clear that Jesus (A.S.) was the last Prophet sent exclusively to the "Children of Israel (i.e. the Jews) and that he was not killed. Further, the Qur'an makes clear that the Prophet Muhammad (saw) was the Prophet which immediately succeeded Jesus (A.S.) and neither was he killed. It is clear that the people of the Scripture referred to, in this verse, were people to whom a number of prophets had come some, of whom were killed. As the Prophet Muhammad (saw) was the last Prophet, of Allah, this verse cannot and does not apply to people who lived after him.

It can then be understood that this verse is speaking about the Jews first, of a past time who had killed prophets and were continuously disobedient to Allah and then about the Jews, of the time of the Prophet Muhammad. While one may not like the Qur'anic characterization, of the Jews, of that time, with whom the Prophet Muhammad (saw) was dealing, as cowards, and those defiantly disobedient, it is historically accurate one borne out by contemporaneous events.

This, of course, does not inform us that for all times, Jews, who had not betrayed their treaties, plotted to kill the Muslims and waged war against the Muslims state, would be forever viewed, in this negative light, but those of what time were and deservedly so.

As was mentioned before when the Prophet Muhammad (saw) first migrated to Madinah from Makkah, he entered, in to a pact, with the people of Madinah, some of whom, where Jews. This pact called for non-aggression and non-participation, in plots and intrigues involving aggression against either party. The Jews, of that time, broke this pact on a number of occasions, and such made themselves eligible, for not only ridicule, but offensive military activities directed against them. What should be of interest to the reader, is what is found, in Leviticus Chapter 26. There, one will find the humiliation and destitution they would suffer if they (i.e. the Jews) opted to reject the commandments of

God (Allah). The language of Leviticus and that of Chapter 3 of the Qur'an are not in conflict. It is doubtful that it can be said that the statements in Leviticus are valid while the same statements, in the Qur'an form some kind of basis for a conspiracy against the Jewish people.

> "And if you are killed, in the cause of Allah, or die – then forgiveness from Allah and Mercy are better than whatever they accumulate (in the world.)
>
> "And whether you die or are killed, unto Allah you will be gathered." Qur'an 3: 157&158

Verses such as these are used by those who oppose Islam, to point to a culture of death, wherein Muslims see no problem with the prospect of killing themselves, in suicide attacks, to affect causality, on their enemies. That, however, is as incorrect as their other claims. Dying, for the sake of Allah, is a noble and praise worthy act irrespective as to what title one places on themselves be that Christian, Jew, Muslim etc. Whoever has sacrificed their lives, in the cause of Allah has achieved the highest form, of righteousness. The Qur'an makes this point clear, in the following verses:

> "And how many a prophet (fought and) with him fought many religious scholars. But they never lost assurance due to what afflicted them, in the cause of

Allah, nor did they weaken or submit. And Allah loves the steadfast."

"And their words where not but they said, "Our Lord, forgive us our sins and the excess (committed) in our affairs and plant firmly our feet and give us victory over the disbelieving people."

"So Allah gave them the reward of this world and the good reward of the Hereafter. And Allah loves the doers of good." Qur'an 3:146-148

So we can dispense with the notion that to be willing, even eager to die, for the sake of Allah, is somehow inherently evil or part and parcel, of a culture of death. Unless, of course, we are now willing to lay this claim on all soldiers who volunteer to go into battle, unless we are going to deny the valor and honor, of those who, in the face of insurmountable odds, give fight to their enemies at the cost of their own lives. If we are willing to accept this as a truth for all people, only then can we look to the Muslims and decry their sacrifice and willingness to die for their faith. That, of course, is separate and distinct from persons, even Muslims, who go out and kill themselves seeking "Martyrdom", and, in the process, kill innocent and the guilty alike.

It is either true that the Qur'an opposes suicide or it does not. Someone making claims the Muslims kill themselves because the Qur'an says that to do so will cause them to enter paradise and receive thereby seventy-two virgins, doesn't make it so. If one makes this claim, we invite them to produce this verse, in the Qur'an supporting their claims. The Muslims assert that the Qur'an contains no such verse and that, in the Qur'an, one may find that which speaks to the prohibition of this act and the promise of the Hell-Fire, for those who ignore this prohibition.

> "o you who have believed, do not consume one another's wealth unjustly but only (in lawful) business by mutual consent. And do not kill yourselves (or one another). Indeed, Allah is to you ever Merciful."

> "And however does that in aggression and injustice – Then We will drive him in to the Fire. And that for Allah is (always) easy." Qur'an 4:28-29

Here Allah has made clear that persons who kill themselves are going to be driven into a fire, as the act is an act of aggression and injustice. Logic would dictate that killing oneself, while at the same time killing others would be a greater act of aggression and injustice. We are fortunate, in that we don't have to rely on logic to tell us this, we need only turn to the Qur'an, in 6:151, 17:33, 25:68&69, to find what means:

"Say 'Come, I will recite what your Lord has prohibited to you. (He commands) that you do not associate anything with Him, and to parents, good treatment, and do not kill your children, out of poverty: We will provide for you and them. And do not approach immorality – what is apparent of them and what is concealed. And do not kill the soul which Allah has forbidden (to be killed) except by (legal) right. This has been instructed you that you may use reason." Qur'an 6:151

"And kill not the soul (i.e. person) which Allah has forbidden, except by right. And whoever is killed unjustly – We have given his heir authority, but let him not exceed limits in (the matter of) taking life. Indeed, he has been supported (by the law)." 17:33

"Those who do not invoke with Allah another deity or kill the soul which Allah has forbidden (to be killed), except by right, and do not commit unlawful sexual intercourse. And whoever should do that will meet a penalty."

"Multiplied, for him, is the punishment, of the Day of Resurrection, and he will abide therein humiliated." Qur'an 25:68 & 69.

Those who say that killing innocent people and killing oneself is forbidden, in Islam have done so having the legitimacy, of the Qur'an to bolster their argument. Those who claim that the Qur'an and Islam Invites to these acts will be required to produce Qur'anic evidence, to the contrary, if they are to be believed, by people possessed of knowledge:

> "Those who believe, fight, in the cause of Allah and those who disbelieve, fight, in the cause of Taghut. So fight against the allies of Satan. Indeed, the plot of Satan, has ever been weak." 4:76

This verse has been used to support the claim that Islam teaches that the Muslim is free to fight against any person who does not belleve in Allah as the One True God, and those who do not hold to what is lawful and prohibited, in Islam. Again returning, to the Qur'an, to explain the verse, we look to the verse which immediately proceeds the verse under discussion, verse 4:75 says what means

> "And what is (The matter) with you that you fight not, in the cause of Allah, and (for) the oppressed among men, women, and children who say, 'Our Lord, take us, out of the city, of oppressive people and appoint, for us, from yourself a protector and appoint for us from Yourself, a helper." 4:75

When verse 76 is read and understood in its full context, one can't help but to understand that its revelation is in relationship to a particular event and that the event involved conduct which was evil. Verse 75 makes it clear that those people who should be fought, should be fought so as to prevent the oppression of men, women and children who want only to be relieved, of their oppression. The event in question, involved people who lived in the city of Makka who were being persecuted for no other reason than they were Muslim. Their Prayer to Allah was answered when an army was raised, Makka was conquered and its people were freed from this oppression. We therefore see that there is a context to this verse that gives lie to the claim that Muslims are free to fight any disbelievers, in Islam, just because they disbelieve, in Islam.

> "They wish you would disbelieve, as they disbelieve so you would be alike. So do not take from among them allies until they emigrate, for the cause of Allah. But if they turn away (i.e. refuse), then seize them and kill them wherever you find them and take not from among them any ally or helper." 4:89

Taken by itself, this verse appears to encourage if not command the Muslims to kill wherever there is found, a group of people refusing to "migrate, in the cause of Allah." It should be noted that here the phrase "migrate in the cause of Allah." means to abandon what Allah has forbidden and embrace righteousness. That notwithstanding, one can read this verse, as some have, and conclude that it is an example of manifest intolerance. This, however, cannot stand when the surrounding verses are read with it. To that end we will add verse 4:88 and 4:90 so that we might place, in to proper context, verse 4:89

> "What is (the matter) with you (that you are) two groups concerning the hypocrites, while Allah has made them fall back (into error and disbelief) for what they earned. Do you wish to guide those who Allah has sent astray? And he who Allah sends astray never will you find for him away (of guidance). 4:88 "They wish you would disbelieve as they disbelieved so you would be alike. Do not take from among them allies until they emigrate for the cause of Allah. But if they turn away (i.e. refuse)., then seize them and kill them wherever you find them and take not from among them any ally or helper," 4:89

> "Except for those who take refuge with a people between yourselves and whom is a treaty or those who come to you, hearts strained at (the prospect of) fighting you or fighting their own people. And if Allah

had willed, He could have given them power over you. So if they remove themselves from you and do not fight you and offer you peace, then Allah has not made for you a cause (for fighting) against them." 4:90

The addition of verses 88 & 89 provide enough context to refute any claims that verse 89 is asking Muslims to engage in transgression, indeed aggression, against a group of people just because they don't believe in Islam. What is of greater explanatory value is a brief review, of the cause, of the verses being revealed?

The Muslims had went out, to the field of battle, a group of 300 hypocrites pretended to be a part of the Muslim force and just prior to the engagement, they left the field, of battle and returned to their homes, leaving short the number of Muslim fighters.

At the conclusion of the battle, two different views emerged from among the Muslims. One view held that the hypocrites should be fought and expelled from their midst, and the second view was that the hypocrites should be left alone. These verses where revealed as a result of these events.

It is doubtful that anyone mindful of the need for unit cohesion in battle situations, can look at these verses and come to a conclusion that they are unfair. Further, the reader will note that verse 90 makes clear that even those traitors and their ilk should not be fought if they themselves either move away to a people who have a treaty with the Muslims or they give up aspirations of fighting the Muslims, and their own people. Verse 89 is blameless with respect to the claims that it invites to unrestricted warfare, wherever such claims arise.

******

We return to the theme that is often shouted, by the enemies of Islam, these claims are that the Qur'an preaches hatred of Christians and Jews. We have dealt with this subject before, and return to it so as to explain the following verses which appears, in a different place, in the Qur'an. When we look to verse 5:51, we find what means:

> "O you who have believed, do not take the Jews and the Christians as allies. They are (in fact) allies of one another. And whoever is an ally to them among you - then indeed,' he is (one) of them. Indeed, Allah guides not the wrong doing people. 5:51

The Christians and Jews, of that time were political enemies of the Muslims. They each were engaged, in some degree, with military aggression against the Muslim state. There can be no difficulty in understanding why the Qur'an commands the Muslims not to take these people as allies. This commandment is not a declaration of war, nor an invitation to aggression.

The next verse we have selected to analyze is, one of three, in the Qur'an, which speaks about a group of Jewish people being turned into apes. This particular verse also includes language where these Jewish people were turned into pigs as well. This writer has had occasion to hear a number of people, say that the Qur'an refers to the Jewish people as Apes and Pigs. This is categorically false, there is not a single verse, in the Qur'an that calls the Jewish people apes or pigs. Let us look at one verse and then the other two, we can then seek the truth surrounding these verses.

> "Say 'Shall I inform you of (what is) worse than that as penalty from Allah? (It is that of) those whom Allah has cursed and with whom He became angry, and made from among them Apes and Pigs and slaves of Tagut.' These are worse, in position and farther astray from the sound way." 5:60

The next verse says what means:

> "And you had already known about those who transgressed among you concerning the Sabbath, and We said to them, "Be apes, despised." 2:55

And the third verse says what means:

"So when they were insolent about that which they had been forbidden, we said to them, "Be apes, despised." 7:1666

The Muslims concede that all of this verse are speaking about Jewish people. Having the three verses together for viewing also reveals that this is not a description of the Jewish people but a punishment that was brought down by Allah on a group of them due to their disobedience. Some Muslim scholars say that this is not a literal punishment, but rather a description, to which the affected people had been subjected. As such they were cursed to behave as apes and pigs. There are other Muslim scholars who say that a group from among them were punished by having been transformed into apes and pigs, having perished without reproducing offspring. We say Allah knows best what He means in these verses. The lesson is clear; disobedience and the transgression of the Sabbath by these Jews was viewed, by Allah, as a great sin and he punished them as a result.

We find it of interest, as well as instructive to look to Biblical text to find what Allah is reported to have said therein regarding this matter.

In Leviticus 26 we find a detailed description of what Allah would do to the Jews if they failed to keep his covenant, which included keeping the Sabbath. I am not certain that a dispassionate reading of these verses would leave the reader with any other conclusion than the punishment that Allah will bring down upon the Jews, was none other than to cause them to become the moral equivalent to wild animals. Leviticus 26 makes clear that those who broke the Sabbath and other commandments would descend in to a state where they would began to eat their young and leave off all civilized, indeed human, behavior. There is but no question that the description of what would happen to a group from among the Sabbath breakers as found, in Leviticus 26, is far worse than what is found in the above three verses of the Qur'an.

*****

The next two verses are also used, by those who seek to distort the Qur'an, in a way that would suggest that the Qur'an gives license to unrestricted warfare. These verses are used more often, by those who are called Islamic Terrorist, than, by those who seek to label Islam as a violet religion. In either case, these claims are defeated when the verses are examined, in their proper context:

> "And let not those who disbelieve think they will escape. Indeed, they will not cause failure to Allah."

> "And prepare against them whatever you are able to of power and of steeds, of war, by which you may terrify the enemy of Allah, and your enemy and others

besides then whom you do not know (but) whom Allah knows. And whatever you spend, to the cause of Allah, will be fully repaid to you, and you will not be wronged." 8:59 & 60

On its face, these verses appear to say that whatever one is able to bring to bear against an enemy, should be brought to bear so that the enemy may be properly terrified, further no expense should be spared in this effort.

If this was the true meaning, of the verses, they would, indeed, be an "Islamic Terrorist's" dream, however, when the verses are examined not, in isolation, but together with other verses that speak to the proper prosecution of war, these verse condemn terrorism, not support it.

No reasonable argument can be made against the provisions that speak to making ready all the power and material that would be needed to defeat an enemy force, for that is the function of any competent military contingent. What is equally true is that terrifying an enemy is a laudable and praise worthy objective, for it lends itself to easier victory and lessens the likelihood of defeated forces re-instituting hostilities. Surely English speaking people around the world are familiar with the phrase "Shock and Awe". Shock and awe sought its objective, to terrify the enemy. One may judge for himself the extent to which they believe it was successful. That notwithstanding, its objective was to sufficiently suppress an enemy force.

What is of value to this discussion, is the portion of the text that says that these efforts are to be addressed to the disbelievers. This appears to be saying that the reason, for engagement and this terrifying of the enemy, is due to their disbelief and not to their having initiated hostilities against the Muslims. However when we look at the verses that proceed the two verses in question, we find the cause for verses 59 & 60 and when we look to verse 61, we find what the Qur'an truly teaches with respect to unrestricted warfare carried out without pause or hesitation.

Verse 8:56-58 discuss a people with whom the Muslims had concluded a treaty, but these same people continually broke their pledge. The Prophet Muhammad (saw) was instructed to dissolve such treaties with people who had given reasons to believe they intended betrayal, it was in this context that 8:59 & 60 were revealed. Let us look at the five verses together.

> "The ones with whom you made a treaty, but then they break their pledge every time, and they do not fear Allah."

"So if you (0 Muhammad), gain dominance over them, in war, disperse by (means of) them those behind them that perhaps they will be reminded."

"If you (have reason to) fear from a people betrayal, throw their treaty back to them, (putting you) on equal terms indeed, Allah does not like traitors.

"And let not those who disbelieve think they will escape. Indeed, they will not cause failure (to Allah.

And prepare against them whatever you are able to of power and or steeds, of war, by which you may terrify the enemy of Allah, and your enemy and others besides them whom you do not know (but) who Allah knows. And whatever you spend, in the cause of Allah, will be fully repaid to you, and you will not be wronged." 8:56-60

It is truly amazing how the meaning of verses changes when the surrounding verses are added. The reader should demand, of anyone, who makes claims that the Qur'an invites to unchecked warfare, that they should not only produce the verse, under discussion, but the surrounding verses as well.

Verse 8:61 follows immediately behind the aforementioned verses and speaks volumes, to the Islamic rules of engagement.

"And If they incline to peace, then incline to it (also) end rely upon Allah. Indeed, it is He who is the Hearing, the Knowing. 8:61

******

Another of the verses of the Qur'an, which is often quoted by those who seek to have the world view Islam as vile and demonic, comes from chapter 8 verse 67.

"It is not for prophet to have captives (of war) until he inflicts a massacre (upon Allah's enemies), in the land. You (i.e. some Muslims) desire the commodities, of this world, but Allah desires (for you) the hereafter. And Allah is Exalted, in Might and Wise 4:67

As the reader can clearly see the words "upon Allah's enemies" are in interpolation, and as such, don't appear in the original Arabic text. As a result, we often find translations that exclude those words causing the text to read something like this "It is not for a prophet to have captives until he has inflicted a massacre in the land." That obviously is a provocative statement which, on its face, begs the question, what kind of religion would require a prophet make slaughter in the land?

We answer this by saying, every religion has required its prophet's to fight in defense of that religion. This verse is making clear to the Prophet Muhammad (saw) and his companions that the objective of any given fight is not to secure worldly gain, in this case, captives whose value lay in the ability to ransom them back to their people but rather to rout the enemy and make clear the way for the people to worship Allah freely, if they so choose. Those who seek to argue with Islam on this point, have a far greater reason to argue with Judaism. That is, if they hold Deuteronomy to be the word of God and a true representation of how Moses (peace be upon him) waged war against the enemies of Allah and the children of Israel.

> "And when the sacred months have passed, then kill the polytheist wherever you find them, and capture them and besiege them and lay, in wait, for them, at every place of ambush. But if they should repent, establish prayer and give Zakah, (wealth due to the poor from the rich) let them (go), on their way, indeed Allah is Forgiving and Merciful." 9:5

Here an opportunity has been presented to make clear a thing which has, for most non-Muslims, been a matter of great misunderstanding. We note that the translation provided for verse 9:5 includes the word "Polytheist", however other translations may use the word "infidels". As a general rule the Qur'an provides for three separate and distinct groups, of non-Muslims, all of whom can correctly be called infidels. What results is a blending of those groups, without distinction, when either of the names, of these groups are translated into English. The Qur'an has addressed these groups as follows: (Kafiruun) disbeliever, (Ahlul Kitaab) People of the Book (that is Christians and Jews) and finally (Mushrik) Pagan or Polytheist.

The problem that arises when the name of these groups are translated as the ubiquitous "Infidel", is that one may read a verse that is speaking exclusively about Idolaters (Mushrik) and apply it to Christian or Jews, or to people who are neither Christian, Jew or Idolater, people who the Qur'an refers to as disbelievers. We note that all the above groups have been referred to, in the Qur'an as disbelievers, but there are occasions when specificity is present, and those verses exclude the other classes of "disbelievers". Such a case can be seen with the verse presently under discussion 9:5.

It has been heard to be said by those who seek to discredit Islam, that this verse applies to all people who are not Muslims, thereby claiming that the Qur'an instructs the Muslims to kill, wherever they are found, those who are considered, by the Muslims, to be infidels. Understanding that this verse specifically addresses idolaters, destroys the validity of any such claim.

Yet, even with the pagans, idolaters and polytheist, this verse is bound by limitations, limitations that are found, in the very next verse which we present presently, Qur'an 9:6:

> "and if any of the polytheist seeks your protection, then grant him protection so that he may hear the words of Allah (i.e. the Qur'an). Then deliver him to his place of safety. That is because they are a people who do not know." 9:6

Again having verse 9:5 read, in its proper context, exonerates it, from the charges that have been leveled against it.

> "And if they break their oaths after their treaty and defame your religion, then fight the leaders of disbelief, for indeed, there are no oaths (sacred) to them: (fight them that) they might cease." 9:12

> "Fight them, Allah will punish them and give victory over them and satisfy the breast (i.e. desires) of the believing people." 9:14

There are those who find it objectionable that the Muslims have, as a right, the ability to target leaders of enemy entities which have broken the covenant with the Muslims, particularly fighting due to defamation. The Muslims, however, offer no apologies for this conduct. Should a people seek to avoid hostilities, then it would be prudent for them to stand by the conditions, of their treaties, and if one of those condition was that they will not attack Islam, in deed or in speech, then failing to abide by those conditions gives license, to the Muslims, to engage their forces and or leaders.

> "Fight those who do not believe, in Allah, or, in the Last Day, and who do not consider unlawful what Allah and His Messenger have made unlawful and who do not adopt the religion, of truth, (i.e. Islam) from those who were given the Scripture (i.e. Christians and Jews) (fight them) until they give the Jizyah willingly while they are humbled." 9:29

This verse is perhaps the one most seized upon as a proof that Muslims are to treat harshly, to the point of fighting and killing, the Christians and the Jews. What is apparent from the verses that have been previous presented, in their full context, is that each of them means something very different than the nefarious interpretation, some would suggest. This is equally true here with respect to verse 9:29.

The verse, of course, appears to be saying that all that is required for the Muslims to engage Christians and Jews, in fight, would be that they don't share the same beliefs as the Muslims. Additionally, that Christian and Jews are to be fought unless and until they become Muslims or pay the Jizyah. The Jizyah being a tax levied on all Christians and Jews and other non-Muslims who have been defeated and or subsequently dwell in Muslim lands, or in lands under Muslim protection. This tax exempts them from the obligation of military service, and they retain the right to practice their religion freely.

While that is the apparent meaning, of the verse, it is an erroneous reading if one seeks to establish that the specificity of the verse, applies to all Christians and all Jews, for all times. Here the verse was revealed in a time when a Christian empire, (i.e. The Romans) and Jewish tribes where engaged in open hostilities, with the Muslim state. This verse addresses the manner, with which these particular people were to be dealt. Yes, this verse also provides guidance, for all time, as to how to deal with Christians and Jews, but only Christian and Jews who are in open hostilities with the Muslims. Such people, according to the Qur'an, are to be fought until they submit to Allah and become Muslim, or they submit to the Muslims, becoming subject to Muslim authority. That is the recompense for unlawful aggression on the part of Christians and or Jews against the Muslims.

> "0 you who have believed, fight those adjacent to you
> of the disbelievers and let them find in you harshness.
> And know that Allah is with the righteous." 9:123

This verse has been used to say that the Qur'an commands the Muslims to fight their neighbors. This, of course, is the position of those who are ignorant. This verse was revealed, in relation to a military expedition, which was conducted by the Muslims against the Byzantine who had decided that the military victories enjoyed by the Muslims over their enemies was a threat to their empire. As a result the Byzantine Empire raised armies with the intention of invading Arabia and, in particular the City of the Prophet (saw) Al-Madinah.

Here, "those near you" means specifically those Byzantine loyalist whose land bordered the lands of the Muslims. We note that, here again, it was not the Muslims who initiated the aggressive activities, rather it was their enemies who did so.

> "Indeed, Allah has purchased from the believers, their lives and their properties (in exchange), for that they will have paradise. They fight, in the cause of Allah, so they kill and are killed. (It is) a true promise (binding) upon Him, in the Torah, and the Gospel, and the Qur'an. And who is truer, to his covenant than Allah? So rejoice, in your transaction, which you have contracted. And it is that which is the great attainment." 9:111

Here, we find a verse that enjoins the believers (i.e. Muslims) to spend generously in the war effort.

This, of course, being the same expedition to be mounted against the Byzantines for their aggression. This verse explains to the believers that they are expected to kill and die when called upon to do so, for the sake of Allah. And in so doing, that they lose nothing but instead they receive the promise of eternal paradise as a result of their sacrifices.

This belies the notion that the Qur'an invites to blood thirst and a feverish pursuit of death. Here there is an address that explains that there is sacrifice, the address recognizing that the believers are giving up something, but that what they give up will be repaid to them as a result of the covenant in which they enter with their Lord, their God, Allah.

******

Looking again at the Qur'an we come across a most beneficial verse. A verse that is in direct conflict with the notion of unrestricted warfare, included in which are many acts of terror. The following verse speaks to the universally held belief, of the right, to self-defense and the near universally excepted position that retaliatory activities form a part of self-defense. In Chapter 16 verse 126 we find the following:

"And if you punish (an enemy), 0 Believers), punish them with an equivalent of that with which you were harmed. But if you are patient, it is better for those who are patient." 16:126"

We also note that the verse is restrictive in nature. It does not allow for disproportionate retaliatory activities, and it goes further to state the beneficial nature of holding patience when wronged, while taking into account human nature to bring harm to those who bring harm to you. The Muslim is confined by this verse, not freed, with respect to carrying out all manner of hostilities.

The very first verses in the Qur'an that allowed for the Muslims to fight their enemies, spoke very specifically to the dangers and ills that would be necessarily present if Allah had not allowed, both the Muslims and former people, the ability to fight those who opposed Allah and His (swt) religion, Al-Islam.

We don't hear very often, the following two verse quoted together by the enemies of Islam. Certainly they will cite the first verse because that verse, without the explanatory context that follows, bolsters their claim that Islam sanctions this notion of unrestricted warfare so popular among those enemies of Islam who target innocent life in the name of Allah. However, a fair reading of either of the verses, even in isolation, will leave the reader with the understanding that the verse is concerned with defense not unprovoked, unrestrained, and indiscriminate offensive activities.

The verses under discussion follows:

> "Permission (to fight) has been given to those who are being fought, because they were wronged. And Indeed, Allah is competent to give them victory." 22:39

When seeking to distort the position that the Qur'an takes on fighting, those inclined to other than the truth, may take this verse, couple it with other verses that touch on the subject and then advance outrageous claims against the Book (i.e. Qur'an). However when the verse that follows (22:39) is added, the discussion necessarily shifts, because this verse destroys their invalid claims. Let us look at the verses, in tandem.

> "Permission (to fight) has been given to those who are being fought, because they were wronged. And indeed, Allah is competent to give them victory." 22:39

> "They are those who have been evicted from their homes without right — only because they say, 'Our Lord is Allah,' And were it not that Allah checks the people some by means of others, there would have been demolished monasteries, churches, synagogues, and Masques, in which the name of Allah, is much

mentioned, (i.e. praised) And Allah will surely support those who support (His cause). Indeed, Allah is powerful end Exalted, in Might." 22:40

Should one seek to critically examine the actions of those calling themselves Muslim, while at the same time bombing Masjids, churches, synagogues and the like, such an examination would reveal these people to be acting in defiance to the Qur'an, not in conformity with it? If verse 22:40 does not make that clear, then we may properly conclude that the reader's bias is so deep, that he cannot be guided by the truth. Surely we have heard it said, "There is none so blind as he who will not see."

******

Another verse, of the Qur'an specifying the rules of engagement, can be found in verse 47:4, but like many of the verses that we have previously discussed if not understood in its proper context, can be used by those wishing to destroy Islam, to mean something very different than it is designed to relate.

Here again interpolation, or the lack thereof, can make the difference in the way this verse is understood by one whose intent is other than to gain guidance. You see, the first sentence in the verse would read like this without interpolation:

"And when you meet the disbelievers, strike necks until you have afflicted slaughter upon them."

This, of course, appears to be a command from the Qur'an to kill any disbeliever that the Muslim meets and that such disbelieving people are to be slaughtered. Glory be to Allah that the verse doesn't end there and when viewed, in full clarity, provides that this activity is part and parcel of armed conflict and not a blanket death warrant as some claim. Before we view the verse, in its entirety, and together with explanatory interpolation, we will first look at the first sentence, of the verse with two words interpolated.

"And when you meet those who disbelieve (in battle) strike (their) necks until, when you have afflicted slaughter upon them."

With the inclusion, of the phrase "in battle" this sentence takes on an entirely different meaning. The reader may say what validates that claim that the verse is, indeed, speaking about "battle" rather than unprovoked, unrestricted and indiscriminate slaughter against non-Muslims? The answer lays in the reading of the entire verse not isolating the above sentence. We find when we read the verse entirety...

"And when you meet those whose disbelieve (In battle) strike (their) neck, until when you have afflicted slaughter upon them, then secure their bonds, and either (confer) favor afterward or ransom (them) until the war lays down it's burden. That (is the Command) and if Allah had willed, He could have taken vengeance upon them (Himself), but (He ordered, armed struggle) to test some of you, by means, of others. And those killed, in the cause of Allah, never will He waste their deeds. 47:4

...it is not necessary to reiterate the Muslim position that claims the right and responsibility to fight against its combative enemies. What is of interest to us here, in this verse, is the intent of the verse and the legally binding mandate found therein. We first note that if the first sentence is understood to mean that the Muslims must go out and slaughter whatever disbelievers he meets, then the rest of the verse ceases to make sense.

For certain, if one is slaughtered he cannot at a later time be shown "favor" nor is he capable of being "ransomed" and most assuredly he represents nothing:, in the way, of harm, necessitating that his "bonds" be "secured". We can properly conclude that all of the above activities are incident, to the proper conduct of war. Secondly the verse mentions those killed, in the cause of Allah. This makes clear that the verse is speaking about conflict wherein both the Muslims and the disbelievers are as likely to be killed.

In any case, the verse read in its entirety speaks to nothing more than certain regulations for armed conflict. All civilized people must have at the center of their war policies, rules that prevent abuses and allow for fair treatment of both their enemies and themselves when taken captive.

How is the reader to understand a verse that explicitly addresses the Prophet Muhammad (saw) and His followers as those who are forceful against the disbeliever? The reader should read such a verse and take it at face value. The reader should know that the Muslims have been commanded to be forceful against the disbeliever. The reader may ask themselves, if this applies to all those who the Muslims call disbelievers, is this directive bond by certain restraints as we have seen, in so many other verses? Let us look at the verse in question.

> "Muhammad is the Messenger of Allah, and those with him are forceful against the disbelievers, merciful among themselves. You see them bowing and prostrating (in prayer), seeking bounty from Allah and (His) pleasure..." 48:29

Can this verse be taken and used to conclude that the Muslims are to treat forcefully, in every circumstances, those who they call disbelievers. The Muslims say no, but what can be produced from the Qur'an that gives clarity to the above verse? Is this forcefulness to be mitigated by circumstances or is its application absolute? Here we utilize the Qur'an to explain the Qur'an using verses 7, 8 and 9 of Surah (chapter) 60 we find:

> "Perhaps Allah will put, between you and those to whom you have been enemies among them, affection and Allah is competent and Allah is Forgiving and Merciful".

> "Allah does not forbid you from those who do not fight you because of religion and do not expel you from your homes from being righteous toward them and act justly toward them. Indeed, Allah loves those who act justly.

> "Allah only forbids you from those who fight you because of religion and expel you from your homes and aid in your expulsion — (forbids) that you make allies of them. And whoever makes allies of them, then it is those who are wrong doers." 60:7, 8 and 9

These 3 verses provides an explanation that speaks to whom, from among the disbelievers, are to be treated "forcefully" and it goes further to speak to whom, from among them, who are deserving of righteous and just treatment from the Muslims. They include the praise of Allah, for those who would treat this category of disbelievers with kindness. What is this category? Those disbelievers who are not fighting against the Muslims and their faith, those not seeking to remove them from their homes nor aiding those people seeking to remove them from their homes.

******

We have attempted, with the foregoing, to give a brief, albeit incomplete, showing of how the verses, in the Qur'an, that deal with fighting with and or treatment of non-Muslims, are grossly distorted and must often quoted and used completely out of their proper context. This by people who have little use for Islam or its tenents.

The verses that were selected for comment largely cover the entire spectrum of the concept of Jihad, in Islam as Jihad relates to fighting. We did not deem it necessary to comment on all the verses that were listed as it would have been redundant. We also note that the verses listed in this chapter do not represent a comprehensive listing of all the verses contained in the Qur'an

57

that deal with the subject, but for the sake of brevity, we listed verses that cover every aspect of fighting, in the cause of Allah.

When the foregoing verses are viewed in light of their proper context, that is to say, a verse either explaining a historical circumstances or giving guidance to the Muslims, as to whom to fight, when to fight, why to fight and how to fight, the verses then begin to take on a meaning very different than is sometimes, presented. They give a message of justice and mercy, not murder and corruption. None of the verses in the Qur'an can be said to condone, command, or invite to the murderous outrages, we see carried out presently, in the name of Islam.

If one can produce a single verse, in the Qur'an that speaks to principles of fighting, that is not accepted by nearly every civilized nation, in the world we invite them to do so. Islam fights to protect its interest at home and abroad. Islam meets its enemies head on, with the aim of killing or capturing as many as can be killed or captured. Islam declares and acts, in accordance, with the right of self-defense. This is all that can be found, in the Qur'an. People who use the Qur'an in an effort to justify that which stretches beyond these principles, have not and do not give the Qur'an its due.

Chapter 2

BIBLICAL VERSES DISTORTED AND DEFAMED

Islam is and should be judged by the book, which purports to be, for the Muslims, the divinely revealed word of God, sent as guidance and to which obedience is a necessary component of belief. This book, of course, is the Qur'an. We have endeavored, in the previous chapter, to present and explain verses of the Qur'an often used to justify the unjustifiable acts of murder and savagery which has quite unfairly come to be known as Islamic terrorism.

The first chapter began a series of steps to demonstrate that Islam has nothing to do with the behavior, of those who carry out acts of terror against civilian populations. Rather, we see a distortion of Islam, using select verses, of the Qur'an and traditions from the Prophet Muhammad (saw), devoid of context, as a justification, for the ravenous, unchecked, unrestricted warfare, which is called terrorism, for the lack of a better term.

Here we would like to look at the book of the Christians, more commonly known as, the Bible. There is neither time nor space, to address the problematic nature of referring to one book as "The Bible", in that different Christian sects have different versions of "The Bible", however, for the purpose of this text, we will use the King James Version, as it is chiefly the version to which most Christians subscribe.

The Muslims believe that their religion should be judged, primarily, on their book. This is because they believe the Qur'an to be the actual word of God to mankind, for proper guidance.

It is fair, fit, and proper to judge Christianity, on its book as well. However, doing so, without seeking to explore and understand the context, in which the book and the verses therein, were revealed, collected and or recorded can and does lead to monumental distortions.

In the present chapter, we do not make any claims or assertions as to what Christianity is or is not, what Christianity invites to or prohibits. We will, instead, select verses, from the Bible and demonstrate that these verse taken, out of context, or without regard to other verses can form the basis for an argument against Christianity being a religion of peace, tolerance and righteousness.

There is a chance that after reading this chapter, we will have succeeded in demonstrating just how easy it is to distort text when people of ill intent, seek to defame the principle holdings, of any given religion.

I must spare no ink, in reiterating that the what follows are not claims to establish the truth of the matter, rather the point, of these claims is to demonstrate one's ability to take, riot only Qur'anic verses, but Biblical verses, as well, and make claims that seem to supported by the text, irrespective as to whether or not these claims are true. This process can be repeated using any written text. It is the hope of this writer, that should anyone seek to use what follows that they have the moral courage and religious integrity to include this paragraph as well.

CLAIM:

Christians believe that the death penalty should be applied to the following offenses: disobedience to parents, homosexuality, murder, debating, backbiting, sex outside of marriage, breaking ones pledge, and lack of compassion. When one finds Christian parents killing their children, it is due to what can be found in the bible.

PROOF:

ROMANS 2:27—32

"and likewise also the men, leaving the natural use of the woman, burned, in their lust one toward another; men with men working that which is unseemly, and receiving, in themselves that recompense of their error which was meet.

"and even as they did not like to retain god in their knowledge, god gave them over to a reprobate mind, to do those things which are not convenient;

61

"being filled with all unrighteousness, fornication, wickedness, covetousness, maliciousness; full of envy, murder, debate, deceit, malignity whispers,

"backbiters, haters of God, despitful', proud, boasters, inventors of evil things, disobedient to parents,

"without understanding, covenant breakers, without natural affections, implacable, unmerciful:

"who knowing the judgment of god, that they which commit such things are worthy of death, not only do the same, but have pleasure in them that do them.

CLAIM:

Jesus (as) sanctioned and commanded the murder of women and children. Because Christians believe that Jesus was always God, as he was the word of God and always with God, they believe that all that God commanded was in fact commanded and

Approved of by Jesus. They hold that whatever was ordered, in the Old Testament is valid and binding on all people, for all time. Whatever is attributed to God, in the Old Testament, is in fact, what must be attributed to Jesus (as).

PROOF:

JOHN 1:1

"in the beginning was the word, and the word was with God, and the word was God."

We note that Christians hold that Jesus is "THE WORD."

MATTHEW 5: 17—19

"think not that i am come to destroy the law, or the prophets, i am not come to destroy, but to fulfill.

"for verily i say unto you, till heaven and earth pass, one jot or one tittle shall, in no wise pass, from the law, till all be fulfilled.

"whosoever therefore shall break one of these least commandments, and shalt teach men so, he shall be called the least in the kingdom of heaven: but whosoever, shall do and teach them, the same shall be called great, in the kingdom of heaven.

The following is what god, which includes Jesus commanded.

DEUTERONOMY 3:3-6.

"so the lord of God delivered unto hand of Og also, the king of Ba'sham, and all his people; and we smite him until none was left to him remaining.

"and cities at that time, there was not a city which we took not from them. Threescore cities, all the region of Ar-gob, the kingdom of Og, in Ba'-shan.

"all these cities were fenced with high walls, gates and bars; beside unwalled towns, a great many.

"and we utterly destroyed them as we did unto Si-hon king of Hesh-bon, utterly destroying the men, women and children, of every city."

The claim is that since Jesus is God and was always God. Then Jesus ordered and approved the killing of innocent women and children. Thereby making it a Christian thing to do.

CLAIM:

Christians believe that god says that any person who divorces and then remarries should be executed.

PROOF:

MATTHEW 5:31

"it hath been said. Whosoever shall put away his wife, let him give her writing of divorcement.

"but i say unto you. That whosoever shall put away his wife, saving for cause of fornication, causeth her to commit adultery: and whosoever shall marry her that is divorced committeth adultery.

We have already provided biblical proofs to establish that the New Testament contains verses that say that persons who commit or cause to be committed, adultery, are "worthy of death" according to the "Judgment of God."

CLAIM:

"Christians who say that Jesus is the only begotten son of God are deliberately lying to the people who they tell this."

PROOF:

PSALMS 2:7

"I will declare that decree: the lord hath said unto me thou are my son: this day have i begotten thee."

This verse is an address to David.

CLAIM:

The bible teaches that it is fit and proper for a man to sell his daughter as a slave.

PROOF:

EXODUS 21:7

"and if a man sell his daughter to be a maidservant, she shall not go out as the menservants do."

Now we move to biblical verses, making no claims as to what they mean, we will, instead, let them stand alone. The reader should read the following verses and understand that these verses are Biblical verses which do not speak to what Christian or Jews profess about their religion. When the reader reads this verses without the benefit of either a Christian or Jew explaining them and or providing some context, distortion will very likely result.

LEVITICUS 20:10

"and the man that committeth adultery with another man's wife, even he that committeth adultery with his neighbour's wife, the adulterer and the adulteress shall surely be put to death.

LEVITICUS 20:13

"if a man also lie with mankind, as he lieth with a woman, both of them have committed an abomination: they shall surely be put to death; their blood shall be upon them."

LEVITICUS 20:14

"and if a man take a wife and her mother, it is wickedness: they shall' be burnt with fire, both he and they: that there be no wickedness among you.

LEVITICUS 20:15

If a man lieth with a beast, he shall surely be put to death, and ye shalt slay the beast.

LEVITICUS 26:27-30

And if ye not for all this hearken unto me, but walk contrary unto me:

Then I will walk contrary unto you also in fury; and I, even I will chastise you seven times for your sins.

And ye shall eat the flesh of your sons, and the flesh of your daughters shalt ye eat.

And I wilt destroy your high places, and cut down your images, and cast your carcasses upon the carcasses of your idols, and my soul shall abhor you.

We note that this description is of a people who have been caused to take on an animal like existence. Not unlike the animal nature of pigs and apes.

EXODUS 21:17

And he that smiteth his father, or his mother, shall be surely put to"death.

EXODUS 22:2—3

If a thief be found breaking up, and be smitten that he die, there shalt be not blood shed for him.

If the sun be risen upon him, there shalt be blood shed for him; for he should make full restitution; if he have nothing, then he shall be sold for his theft.

EXODUS 22:20

he that sacrificeth unto any god save unto the lord only, he shall be utterly destroyed.

Would it at all be fair to say that the Bible tells it's followers to kill everyone who performs acts of worship to any god, other than the God of the Bible?

DEUTERONOMY 3:33 &34

And the lord our God delivered. Him before us; and we smote him, and his sons, and all his people.

And we took all his cities at that time, and utterly destroyed the men, and the women, and the little ones, of every city, we left none to remain.

What kind of unfounded and damaging claims can be raised against the Bible, if only these two verse were used to speak to the message of the Bible?

DEUTERONOMY 12:1—3

These are the statutes and judgements, which ye shall observe to do in the land, which the lord god of thy fathers giveth thee to possess it, alt the days that ye live upon the earth.

Ye shall utterly destroy all the places, wherein the nations which ye shalt possess served their gods, upon the high mountains and upon the hills, and under every green tree.

And ye shall overthrow their altars, and break their pillars, and burn their groves with fire; and ye shall hew down the graven images of their gods, and destroy the names of them out of that place.

DEUTERONOMY 13:1—10

If there arise among you a prophet, or a dreamer of dreams, and giveth thee a sign or a wonder,

And the sign or the wonder come to pass, whereof he spake unto thee, saying, let us go after other gods, which thou hast not known, and let us serve them;

Thou, shall not hearken unto the words of that prophet, or that dreamer of dreams: for the lord your God proveth you, to know whether ye love the lord your God with all your heart and with all your soul.

Ye shall walk after the lord your God, and fear him, and keep his commandments, and obey his voice, and ye shall serve him, and cleave unto him.

And the prophet, or that dreamer of dreams, shall be put to death: because he hath spoken to turn you away from the lord your god, which brought you out of the land of Egypt, and redeemed you out of the house of bondage, to thrust thee out of the way which the lord thy God commanded thee to walk in. So shalt thou put the evil away from the midst of thee.

If thy brother, the son of thy mother, or thy son, or thy daughter, or the wife of thy bosom, or they friend, which is as thine own soul, entice thee secretly, saying, let us go and serve other gods, which thou hast not known, thou, nor thy father;

Namely, of the gods of the people which are round about you, nigh unto thee, or far off from thee, from the one end of the earth even unto the other end of the earth;

Thou shalt not consent unto him, nor hearken unto him; neither shall thine eye pity him, neither shalt thou spare, neither shalt thou conceal him:

But thou shalt surely kill him; thine hand shall be first upon him to put him to death, and afterward the hand of all the people.

And thou shalt stone him with stones, that he die; because he hath sought to thrust thee way from the lord thy God which brought thee out of the land of Egypt, from the house of bondage.

DEUTERONOMY 21:18—21

If a man have a stubborn and rebellious son, which will not obey the voice of his father, or the voice of his mother, and that, when they have chastened him, will1 not hearken unto them:

Then shall his father and his mother lay hold on him, and bring him out unto the elders of his city, and unto the gate of his place;

And they shall say unto the elders of his city, this our son

Is stubborn and rebellious, he will not obey our voice; he is a glutton, and a drunkard.

And all the men of his city shall stone him with stones, which he die: so shalt thou put evil away from among you; and all Israel shall hear, and fear.

DEUTERONOMY 25:5—6

If brethren dwell together, and one of them die, and have no child, the wife of the dead shall not marry without unto a stranger: her husband's brother shall go into her, and take her to him to wife, and perform the duty of a husband's brother unto her.

And it shall be, that the firstborn which she beareth shall succeed in the name of his brother which is dead, that his name be not put out of Israel.

NUMBERS 21:32-35

And Moses sent to pay out Jaazer and they took the villages thereof, and drove out the Amorites that were there

And they turned and went up by the way of Bashan and Og and the king of Bashan went out against them, he and all his people, to the battle of Edrel.

And the lord said unto Moses, fear him not: for I have delivered him into thy hand, and all his people, and his land: and thou shalt do to him as thou didist unto Sihon king of the Amorites which dwelt at Heshbon

So they smote him, and his sons, and all his people, until there was none left him alive; and they possessed his land.

Here, wherever a claim has been raised, however ridiculous or absurd, it may be, it is supported by the evidence found, in these biblical verses, and yet it cannot be found that either the Christians of the Jews hold these claims to be truthful. We can fairly say that, in the main, they don't believe these claims, nor do they teach these claims. That being said, there can be no question that there are those from amongst the followers of the Bible who take it to be the literal word of God, who believe and teach that both the Old and New Testaments must, be taught and followed to the letter. The question that arises is what can be gained by judging the whole of Judaism and Christianity by the views of these few?

It is our hope that the honest reader can understand that Non-Muslims are not permitted to make definitive claims as to what Islam invites to, unless they study Islam and all of the evidence used in Islam to make edicts. Just as it is inappropriate for non-Christians to say what Christianity calls to, unless the same study is undertaken, with respect to Christian texts.

One can't go to the Qur'an, extract verses from here and there and from that make unfounded claims that Islam, the Qur'an, and the Muslims, invite to indiscriminate violence against Non-Muslims or any other atrocities (i.e. terrorism). It matters not if persons engaged, in this abhorrent practice, claims a faith other than Islam or claims that they themselves are Muslim. In the end they defame people of faith, and prove themselves to be little more than liars.

I have taken the decision not to put in this chapter the Jewish or Christian beliefs (as they are known to me) concerning these claims and other verses, because to do so would diminish the impact of the distortion. Should one seek to understand what Christians or Jews truly believe about these verses, they will need to investigate the truth of the matter for themselves. Which is what should be done when the reader sees claims made against Islam, the Qur'an, and the Muslims.

Chapter 3

THE PROPHET MUHAMMAD (SAW)

HIS SUNNAH, AND JIHAAD

There was an effort in the first chapter, to briefly expound upon the Islamic belief that the primary sources of law in Islam are two and that all other sources of law derive from these two primary conduits. We have said that these sources are The Qur'an, which the Muslims believe is the literal and unaltered word of Allah (God) sent to the Prophet Muhammad (saw) through the Angel Jabriel (Gabriel) (AS). Muslims believe it to be inimitable and incorruptible. The second of those two sources is the Sunnah.

This, the Sunnah, can be described as law which is formulated based on the commandments, prohibitions, sayings and or actions of the Prophet Muhammad ibn Abdullah (saw). We note that this too was sent down by Allah (swt) to the Prophet (saw), so that the Sunnah is divine revelation as well.

To put the matter into lay terms, the Sunnah is the body of evidence that explains how the Prophet Muhammad (saw) himself, understood and therefore acted on Allah's commandments, prohibitions and dictates. It is from observing how he, the Prophet (saw), responded to these things, that we know with certainty how it is the Muslims are to respond.

The term Sunnah has a number of different Shariah (legal) meanings, this is not the time nor place for elucidation of those meanings. Here, we will confine ourselves to the two defin1ton that will allow us to understand and approach the discussion of terrorism as it relates to the Religion of Islam. As such we will use the above definition to establish that the Sunnah is one of two sources of law. The second definition will be very similar to our first definition. We have said that one definition of Sunnah is law which is derived from the actions and saying of the Prophet Muhammad and here we say that another definition, indeed, a second definition, speaks not to the legality of those action or sayings but simply asserts there existence. That is to say that another definition of Sunnah is simply, the actions, sayings, commandments, prohibitions, approvals and disapprovals, both tacit and direct, of the Prophet Muhammad (saw). I apologize for the wordy, if not academic nature of this explanation, but I find it necessary, if there is going to be a true understanding of the points that follow.

When the Muslims look for a behavioral model, they look to the Prophet Muhammad (saw), when seeking to gain an understanding of how he or she should behave in a particular circumstance, and or what is the proper Islamic position regarding a particular issue, the Muslims looks first to what has reached him from the Prophet Muhammad (saw) concerning the matter. The proof of the correctness of this approach is found in the Qur'an:

> "There has certainly been for you in the Messenger of Allah, en excellent example, for anyone whose hope is, in Allah and the Last Day, end (who) remembers Allah often?" Qur'an 33:21

Given this understanding, the best way to understand what Islam says about Jihaad and how it is that the Muslims are to approach Jihaad, is to look to what the Prophet Muhammad (saw) has said, done, commanded, prohibited, and allowed with respect to Jihaad. Similarly, we can look to the Prophet (saw) to understand what Islam teaches concerning the treatment of fellow human beings, be they Muslim or otherwise.

It needs to be established that Muslims have a religious obligation to follow the guidance, of the Prophet Muhammad (saw), or put another way they are obligated to and confined, by the Sunneh. This can only he established with irrefutable proofs, we offer a few here.

We begin with the Qur'an, we cite a verse where Allah (swt) explains why the Qur'an was revealed to the Prophet Muhammad (saw), and what is the position, (according to Allah (swt) of the Prophet, in relationship, to the Qur'an.

"And We have not revealed to you the Book (0 Muhammad), except for you to make clear to them that wherein they have differed and as guidance an Mercy for a people who believe." Qur'an 16:64

Here, we find that Allah (swt) has told the Muslims that the reason that the Book was revealed to Muhammad (saw) was so that he, Muhammad (saw) could explain to the Muslims and others the true meaning of things about which there was some difference of opinion, and to further offer guidance to the Muslims as to how to behave and what constitutes, true faith. Should a Muslim seek to understand the Qur'an, in a way that differs from the way it was understood and explained, by the Prophet Muhammad (saw), then he does so, in defiance to the above quoted verse.

We again return, to the Qur'an, seeking proof that the Muslim is obligated to follow the Sunnah, of the Prophet Muhammad (saw). There are no verses, in the Qur'an, were Allah has commanded obedience to himself, except that, in that same verse Allah has commanded obedience, to His Messenger (saw). No Muslim claims or holds the belief that he or she is free to disobey or disregard what has been commanded of them, by Allah. In the Qur'an Allah equates obedience to the Prophet (saw), with obedience, the Himself (swt). We find:

"He who obeys the Messenger has obeyed Allah; but those who turn away, We have not sent you over them as a guardian." Qur'an 4:80

Again, one seeking to claim that he is not required to obey what the Prophet Muhammad (saw) has commanded or prohibited, will have to make such a claim while rejecting verse 4:80, which is effectively rejecting the revealed word of Allah. May Allah save us from this destructive deed?

There are a great number of prophetic traditions which form a part of the Sunnah, speaking to this obligation, but it is not necessary, in this case, to go beyond what Allah has revealed, in the Qur'an.

It is hoped the reader has come to understand that the only true way to understand Islam is to understand Islam, in the way, in which it was understood and practiced, by the Prophet of Islam, the Prophet Muhammad (saw). This is the view, of the Muslims, who follow the Qur'an and the Sunnah of the Prophet Muhammad (saw). Those who do not follow the Qur'an and the Sunnah of the Prophet Muhammad (saw), are left to explain how they reject this practice given the verses we have previously quoted, in this chapter.

Given that, let us look to what the Prophet of Islam has said about Islam as it relates to Jihaad. We shall, Insha'Allah, examine

Prophetic traditions, on the subject, in an effort, to determine, first; if Islam invites to acts of terror and second; weather or not those acting, in the name of Islam, are in fact, acting in accordance with the commandment and prohibitions of the Prophet of Islam (saw).

The Ahadeeth (Prophetic traditions) which follow are taken from books of hadeeth found, in the chapters that deal with Jihaad, military campaigns and good manners. Taken as a whole they help to shed light, on the Prophet Muhammad's (saw) view, of these subjects.

****

The following hadeeth demonstrates quite clearly that Jihaad, in Islam, has a goal. It is not focused on killing just for the sake of killing. Jihaad, as we have mentioned before, is for the purpose of securing the right of people to worship Allah in the way He (swt) has commanded he be worshiped or to reject this worship and worship as he wishes. This is somewhat complicated when one seeks to understand this concept through western eyes. Worshiping Allah as one wishes does not mean that one is free to "make up a god" and then worship the created or fabricated thing. Islam was sent to oppose such practices.

Even once the decision has been taken to raise an army and engage an enemy force, this goal is still the primary objective. Not killing and conquering, but to invite to Allah and Allah alone as the only deity worthy of worship.

The companion, of the Prophet (saw) Sahl ibin Sa's (RA) reported that he heard the Prophet Muhammad (saw) say on the battle of Khaibar:

> "I will give the flag to a person at whose hand Allah will grant victory," so the companions, of the Prophet (saw,) got up, wishing eagerly to see to whom the flag will be given, and every one of them wished to be given the flag. But the Prophet (saw) asked for Ali (RA). Someone informed him that he was suffering from eye trouble. So, he ordered them to bring 'Ali (RA), in front of him.

Then the Prophet (saw) spat, in his eyes, and his eyes were cured immediately as if he had never any eye trouble. Ali said, "We will fight with them (i.e. Infidel) till they become like us (i.e. Muslim). The Prophet (saw) said: "Be patient, til you face them and invite them to Islam and inform them of what Allah has enjoined upon them. By Allah! If a single person embraces Islam at your hands (i.e. through you) that will be better, for you than the red camels." Sahih Bukhari# 1266

There are those who will take this hadeeth and claim that it provides proof that Islam is spread through the sword. We respond by saying that it has never been a Muslim claim that Islam is not sometimes spread, by the sword, but this is true of every sociopolitical system. Islam, while being viewed, by some, as a religion is, in truth, not just a religion, but an entire way of living. A system complete with its own values and norms; a system designed to impact and inform the lives of those who live under its sway.

People say that Islam was spread, by the sword, as if that was inherently evil. The United States of America, together with Great Briton, and the "Coalition of the willing," are currently engaged, in military activities designed to bring democracy to the Islamic world through its experiments, in Afghanistan and Iraq. They are not seeking to sway the people to the way of democracy with the Bible. They have in fact made use of the force of arms to permit the people of those nations to raise their voices and choose for themselves what they will and will not follow.

Who of sound mind and understanding, can claim that anything different is true of Islam when force is necessary because freedom to worship Allah is barred? The Americans fight and kill for democracy, because the spread of democracy is in its interest, in most cases. So too, do the Muslim fight and kill not for democracy, but so that the religion of Allah may reign supreme, so that those who wish to worship Allah and live in accordance with the laws of Allah are free to do so without interference from individuals or governments. So the Muslim has no problem with the assertion that Islam was spread by the sword, for that is in part true. However, where there exist criticism, there needs to be criticism for every world power past and present.

*****

There once was a man who came to the Prophet Muhammad (saw) and asked permission to go forth in Jihaad. Upon this the Prophet (saw) asked.

> "Are your parents alive?" He replied in the affirmative. The Prophet (saw) said to him, "Then exert yourself, in their service."

This hadeeth shows that Jihaad is not to be the primary focus of the Muslim's life, not only that but it shows that Jihaad is not an objective, in and of itself. Here this man was asked whether or not his parents were alive and when it became known that they were, the Prophet (saw) told the man what means: "Go forth in Jihaad by taking care of them." What can be known from this is that Jihaad is accomplished not only, on the field, of battle, but also in ones (everyday life, that Jihaad is only Jihaad fis sabilil lah (struggle, in the cause of Allah), when the objective, is righteousness. This was the attitude, of the Prophet of Islam, Muhammad ibn Abdullah (saw).

In recent times, it has been reported that Az-Zakawi, the leader of Al-Qaidah in Iraq, has said that he and all Muslims are opposed to democracy and any person who participated in the Iraqi elections of January 2005, would be subject to having their heads cut off and those of their children. Az-Zakawi, if these statements are true, was speaking to Muslims and non-Muslims alike. His Proclamation was that all persons having participated in these elections where now enemies of Allah and Islam, and thereby making their blood lawful and the blood of their children became lawful as well. We thank Allah that Az-Zakawi now stands before the One True Judge, and his evil is no more.

This notion as expressed by Az-Zakawi is rejected by the Muslim collective. It is true, that Western style democracy is forbidden in Islam, and that no Muslim, of true faith, can embrace such a system except while having rejected, in part, the teachings of the Quran, and those found in the Sunnah. That of course, is very different from one claiming that Muslims who participate in and or embrace any form of democracy are enemies of Islam, making their blood lawful to shed. (Democracy and its relationship to Islam will be discussed in the last chapter).

In examining the two following hadeeth, even the most inherently hostile detractor of Islam will have to admit, that with respect to evidence, that Az-Zakawi and those who believe as he does are completely outside of the bounds of Islam, as explained and practiced by the Prophet of Islam (saw).

> Narrated As-Sab bin Jaththanma (RA). The Prophet (saw) passed by me at a place call Al—Abwa or Waddan, and was asked whether it was permissible to attack Al—Mushrikun (Polytheist, Pagans) warriors at night with the probability of exposing their women and children to danger. The Prophet (saw) replied, "They (i.e. women and children) are from them... (i.e. Pagans) Summarized Bukhari P.612 #1292

It is certain that there exists, some level of ambiguity, in this hadeeth, for there is not clarity as to how the women and children are to be treated. Here we find that it is permissible to engage an enemy force even if doing so necessarily means that the non-combative women and children may be killed or maimed as a result. What is not present, in this hadeeth, is clarity as to whether or not the women and children are permitted to be targeted because they belong to a people who are being engaged by Muslim forces.

One, so inclined, can take this hadeeth and say that because the women and children are from among them (i.e. the enemy) then they too can be treated as a combatant. Such an interpretation would have to be formed while ignoring two key evidentiary points. First that the hadeeth contains clarifying language with respect to whom permission is being sought to fight, women and children are excluded from that questioning. Clarity as to legality of fighting combative forces was being sought, the condition which was unclear to the questioner was whether it was lawful to engage these combatants, if hurting women or children could result. He did not ask whether or not it was lawful to target the woman and children. Secondly he, the one who seeks to kill women and children, would be ignoring the other hadeeth, on the subject.

When we look to the second hadeeth we find out what was the position, of the Prophet Muhammad (saw) with respect to killing women and children.

> Narrated Abdullah bin'Umar (RA) during some Ghazawaat (Battle in which the Prophet himself participated) of the Prophet (saw) a woman was found killed. Allah's Messenger (saw) disapproved the killing of women and children." Summarized Bukhari P.613 #1293

Here, in this hadeeth, we find that the companions of the Prophet (saw) were informed, of the prohibition of killing women and children. Taken alone one can take this hadeeth and say that Muslims are not permitted to engage an enemy force and even accidentally kill women and children. The Muslims, of course, do not seek to understand a practice of the Prophet (saw) by isolating one of his sayings, but rather taking all of his sayings as a whole, it is from this amalgamation, that the Muslim comes to properly understand how he is to approach a given circumstance.

This hadeeth makes clear that women were killed in battles, as the hadeeth mentions multiple battles where a woman was observed killed. The hadeeth also asserts that it is understood that the killing of women and children is a prohibited act. The hadeeth does not give us any understanding if the woman was killed with a stray arrow or spear, if she was failed by her own people, if she had produced a weapon, so one cannot speak to whether or not she was killed intentionally or by mistake. What is of importance, is that the sight of a dead women, on the field of battle, was noteworthy and a sight which brought to mind the prohibition against killing women and children intentionally.

How do the threats of Az-Zakawi and his ilk stand, in the face, of the prophetic traditions? If there are those who claim that threatening, and in some cases, killing Iraqi children, whether

Muslim or not, is an act sanction by Islam, let him produce authentic proof to substantiate his claim. For certain, such a one would have to assert that the Prophet of Islam permitted killing non-combative women and children. If this is truthful, he will not have a problem producing authentic proof to demonstrate even a single circumstance where the Prophet (saw) either engaged in, or sanctioned this practice.

******

This next hadeeth gives us not only an opportunity to speak to how the Prophet (saw) understood, the issue of unrestricted warfare, but also the necessity to confront excesses when they become known.

> "Narrated 'Ikrima (RA) Ali burnt some people and this news reached Ibn Abbas (RA) and he said, "Had I been in his place I would not have burnt them, as the Prophet (saw) said 'Don't punish (anybody) with Allah's Punishment' No doubt, I would have killed them, for the Prophet (saw) said, 'If somebody (a Muslim) discards his religion, kill him." Summarized Buhkhari P613 #1294

As it relates to the notion that Islam invites to and sanctions unrestricted warfare, this hadeeth belies that claim. Here we find that one of the companions of the Prophet (saw) repudiated the unlawful aspect of All's behavior and affirmed what he knew to be from the Prophet (saw). This is the way of Islam, the way of the Muslim.

If the Muslim was permitted to decide for himself how to kill and how not to kill, then Ibn Abbas would have had no call to speak about the conduct of Ali. Instead we find that Ibn Abbas said that he would not have done this act as it was an act that was contrary to what he knew to be from the guidance of Allah' Messenger (saw).

We can imagine that if Ibn Abbas had been present when Ali (RA) had these people burnt, he would have told Ali (RA) not to commit this act for the act was a transgression against the rights of Allah. The only way that Ali (RA) would have been permitted to proceed with this act, in the face of the Prophet's prohibition, would have been with proof that the Prophets (saw) did, in fact, permit this practice.

This hadeeth speaks to limitation on one's ability to carry out justice. When acting on behalf of Allah and His (swt) Deen (religion), one must stay within the confines of what he is permitted. He is not permitted to kill as he pleases, even when those being killed are deserving of death.

Ibn Abbas affirmed that those who leave the religion of Islam should be killed. The Muslim should not spend too much time defending this position. All nations punish traitors harshly, some prescribe death others imprisonment. What is of import here is that Ibn Abbas condemned what he felt was a lack of restraint, on the part of Ali (Ra), while affirming that the act of killing these apostates was lawful and as such should have been accomplish, by lawful means.

******

We have asked the reader to consider that war in Islam is not an objective, in and of itself, hut rather serves a greater purpose of freeing obstacles to the proper worship of Allah (swt). We have said that warfare in Islam does not seek to destroy all before it without mercy or discrimination. The Hadeeths that follow gives weight to that argument. We find therein proof that in war the Muslim may take captive those wounded or who surrender, they also engage the practice of returning the enemy force to their people for a price. This a reciprocal practice, by which Muslim soldier are also returned when captured.

Narrated Abu Musa (RA) The Prophet (SAW) said, "Free the captives feed the hungry and pay a visit to the sick." Summarized Bukhari P. 618 #1301

> Narrated Abu Huraira (RA): "A man said to the Prophet (SAW) "Advise me!" The Prophet (saw) said, "Do not become angry and furious," The man asked (the same) again and again and the Prophet (saw) said in each case, "Do not become angry and furious." Summarized Bukhari P. 962 #2042

I'm not certain how people claiming Islam as their faith, can do what has been prohibited in Islam, and use as a justification for these acts their outrage at their enemies' conduct, while at the same time these people claim to give full faith and credit to the above hadeeth. A scant few hadeeth that speak to the need of the Muslims to act justly have been mentioned here, yet they clearly began to paint a picture of the teachings of Islam that are directly contrary to indiscriminate killing and unrestricted warfare.

How is it that one can be said to be obligated to kill his neighbor when his Prophet has commanded kindness to neighbors? How do we say that it is permitted for the Muslim to target non-combatants, men women or children, when the Prophet of Islam, the one who brought the religion, the one whom the Muslims are obligate to follow, has forbidden the act? It should becoming clear to the reader that people who are engaged in killing for the sake of killing, cannot be said to be doing so for the sake of Allah or

Allah's religion. It should become clear to the reader, that Islam is indeed a religion, of peace.

That notwithstanding, there are certainly those who remain unconvinced that Islam does not teach, advocate or endorse the targeting of non-combatants. We shall, Insha'Allah, provide more evidence of what the Prophet of Islam, did teach, did advocate and did in fact, endorse.

There are those who seek to apologize for what Allah (swt) has revealed, in the Qur'an, as it relates to fighting, the same people seek to apologize for or explain in unacceptable terms the methods employed by Allah's Messenger (swt), the Prophet Muhammad (saw), no such effort will be forth coming here.

Islam is undoubtedly unpalatable to some people. There are a variety of reasons for this, one of which is Islam's insistence that Jihaad, (fighting in the cause of Allah) is an obligation, on every able bodied male Muslim, on the planet. Most people, Muslims and non-Muslims alike, do not properly understand Jihaad, and we know that people fear what they do not understand.

In the previous chapter there was mention, of the need for the Muslims to make sure that people are free to worship Allah (God) if they choose to do so. We, of course, recognized that people find it strange that a means to ensure that the worship of Allah (swt) is available, in an unfettered fashion, is to kill on the field of battle, those who would deny people this free and unfettered access to Allah (swt). While we understand that there are those who disagree, we recognize that uniformity and consensus is rarely seen on any matter and it has never been found to exist on matters of religion. That notwithstanding, Islam does not shrink from the call to arms, when the call to arms becomes necessary to defend or provide real access to the faith.

Nations of the world fight and kill to defend their interest and to spread whatever political ideology they may espouse. They do so, most often, at the time and place of their choosing for reasons that often make sense to only themselves. Trying to convince those opposed to their aggression and expansions of the correctness of their acts is, at best, an exercise in futility. Just as if would be a futile effort to try to convince non-Muslims that the Muslims are correct in fighting people for the purpose of making Allah's word supreme.

Time would be better spent advancing the argument that while others may not think it a proper activity, that the Muslims are not deviating from the accepted and common practices of the world's leading powers, past or present. So when we find a hadeeth that says:

> Abu Muse (RA) narrated: A man came to the Prophet (saw) and asked, "0 Messenger of Allah, a man fights for booty, another fights for fame, and a third fights, for showing off, which of them is in the cause of Allah?" The Messenger of Allah (saw) said, "He who fought so that the word of Allah (swt) remains superior, is the one who fought in the cause of Allah." Summarized Sahih Muslim) P. 554 #1088

We note upon finding such hedeeth, that the Messenger of Allah, is not advocating the killing of non-Muslims just because they don't believe in Allah. Rather what he is saying is that when the Muslims, in accordance with their interest, and the advancement of their sociopolitical/religious ideology, and at the time and place of their choosing engage an enemy force, the reason for such engagement should be for the purposes of advancing Allah's agenda on earth. This hadeeth also makes clear that any other motivation is rejected, by Allah, as being done for His (swt) sake.

In modern warfare, among the armies of Muslims, and non-Muslims alike, there exists an atmosphere and belief that soldiers, when they go to war, are heroes, their motivations notwithstanding. In modern times, indeed, in all times, individual motivation for one's service in a fighting force was not questioned. One is considered equally brave if he is motivated to fight out of a desire to defend his nation or faith, as he would be if his fighting was incidental and as result of his desire to advance his military, political, or civilian career.

That is not true of Islam. Both the aforementioned hadeeth and the one that follows demonstrates that the Muslims motivations for fighting must be free of desire for personal advancement either by way of showing off, for fame, or fortune. It is proper to ask what motivations can be ascribed to people who behead their fellow human beings in a manner most suitable to sheep, then post these executions on the Internet proclaiming to the world who they are.

We quote the following hadeeth, in relevant parts:

> Sulaiman bin Yasar reported: People dispersed from around Abu Hurairah (RA) and Natil, who was from the Syrians said to him: "0 Shaikh, give us a tradition which you heard from the Messenger of Allah (saw) say "The first man whose case will be decided on the Day of Resurrection, will be a man who dies as a martyr. He shall be brought forth, and Allah will recount His blessing upon him and he will recognize them. Then Allah (swt) will say: 'What did you do with them? He will say: "I fought in your cause and was killed as martyr.' Allah will say: "You lie, your fought to be called a brave warrior, And you were

called so!' Then he will be ordered to be dragged, on his face into Hell." Summarized Muslim PP.554—555 1089.

Where, in the above language, do we find room for one to interpret that if one kills himself even having done so to kill his enemy that he will be granted paradise? It is difficult to believe that such a belief can exist, in light of this hadeeth. Here a man who was to all who saw him a brave warrior, yet Allah put him in the Hell-Fire because he was not motivated by fighting to make Allah's word supreme.

How can one who kills the children of his enemy, at the same time invite that enemy to a better way? How can it be expected that the enemy will forgive this outrageous trespass and embrace, in truth, that to which you invite him? Logic and reason informs us that terrorist cannot be working to make the Word of Allah supreme when their tactics are that of indiscriminate killing, savage be-headings and incinerating non-combatant men, women, and children alive. There is great difficulty in understanding the Justice of a God who places, in the Hell-Fire, a man who has only killed Allah's enemies yet permits to enter paradise those who have taken life which He (swt) has made sacred. Indeed, it is Allah who is the Most Just of Judges.

There exists, in the following hadeeth, a most amazing example of Allah's Messenger's (saw) rejection of unrestricted warfare, and of the notion that all is fair in war. What we find instead, is the Messenger of Allah (saw) acting, in ways that appear to be to his own detriment, the detriment, of the Muslims and Islam, when abandonment of ethics and guidelines would seem to have been a more prudent course. In truth, this great man understood the importance of being true to Allah and faithful to one's covenant.

In the battle of Badr, the Muslims were outnumbered nearly 4 to 1 as the Muslims had just over 300 fighters and the Quraish (the enemy army) had over 1300. Yet when confronted with a choice between adding to the number of the Muslim fighters and being true to a covenant, the Messenger of Allah (saw) chose the latter. We read:

> Hudhaifah bin Al-Yaman (RA) said: Nothing prevented me from being present at the battle of Badr except this incident. I came out with my father Husail to participate, in the battle, but we were caught, by the disbelievers, of Quraish. They said, "Do you intend to go to Muhammad?" We said. "We do not Intend to go to him, but we wish to go back to Al-Madinah." So they took from us a covenant, in the name of Allah, that we would go back to Al-Madinah and would not

fight on the side of Muhammad (saw). So, we came to the Messenger of Allah (saw) and related the incident to him. He said: "Both of you proceed to A1-Madinah, we will fulfill the covenant made with them and seek Allah's help against them" summarized Muslim P.573 #1125.

The behavior and instruction of Allah's Messenger (saw) does not, in any way, seem compatible with the conduct of those who seem to believe that an "Anything goes" mentality is part and parcel of the Islamic faith. A fair minded reader has been provided with more than enough proof that Islam is not a religion that calls to or for blood thirsty revenge, nor is it a religion that approves wanton murder, nor unrestricted warfare. Those people who continue to make this call, in light of this evidence, cannot be said to be other than people without reason. If one occupies a belief that differs from what is found in these pages this writer invites such a one to produce some evidence from sound Islamic sources that belies our claims.

We would do well to learn to separate the actions of Muslims from the teachings of Islam. There is clear certainty that should one seek to examine any of the world's great religions, in light of what its followers have done rather than what the text teaches, one would quite easily conclude that by comparison so called Islamic terrorism, doesn't even register, on the scale of atrocities.

Chapter 4

UNTIL THE WAR LAYS DOWN ITS BURDEN

WHY ISLAM WILL ALWAYS BE AT WAR WITH THE WEST

Islam stands apart from the rest, of the world's religions, in that Islam, is completely reliant upon textual evidence to establish its tenants. There is no human involvement, in this process, except by way of reading what has been revealed, by Allah (swt), in the Qur'an, as it relates to these tenants and or the reading of the Prophetic traditions as they relate to the same. It is not possible for a scholar or any other religious leader to Supply an Interpretation of Islamic tenants that go beyond, or differ in any way from that which has reached us from the Messenger of Allah (saw). That, of course, being Muhammad ibn Abdullah (saw). For this reason the question as to whether or not Islam can be compatible with any system of government, save Islamic Shari'ah, is a textual one and cannot be reached by application of human logic or reasoning, though these means must be employed to understand the question.

The perfect reality is that Islam must always apply its sacred text, in coming to any decision that affects the lives of the Muslims as a whole. To the extent that this text (i.e. Qur'an) does not conflict with the principles that are laid out in a particular system of governance, the Muslim is free to follow such laws or principals. This, of course, because Islam is derived in the minds of the Muslims, from the divinely revealed Word of Allah (swt) and the practices of Allah's messenger (saw). There exist no possibility that man, using his logic and reason, his life experiences, and limited foresight, will be able to come up with a system as perfect as the system which is derived from the Wisdom of Allah (swt), The All-Mighty, The All-Knowing. It is therefore, safe to say that at a bare minimum, any system not Islamic Shariah will conflict in some appreciable fashion with Islamic Shari'ah.

Conflict, with respect to Allah's (swt) law is by definition, incompatible with Allah's law. Since Islam is nothing more than the systematic, regimented, ritualized practice of Allah's (swt) law, Islam can never be compatible with any other system of governance. This being a fact which is manifestly salient, the question arises as to what does it mean vis-avis Islam, and the rest of the world?

With noted exceptions, Islam's chief adversaries are Western/European nations, of which the United States is included. Those nations which have adopted Western /European models of governance, by virtue of their conduct toward Muslims, are often times include among the adversaries, of Islam. That is to say that, where major conflicts exist with Islam, it is almost invariably, with democracies, or regimes being propped up by democracies.

There is no possibility of there every being any synergy or compatibility between Islam and Western style democracies. That is the extent to which Islam and Western style democracies differ. There exist now and will forever exist a fundamental conflict between the Islamic mind and that of the Democrat. The Democrat believes that man should be free to choose, his own destiny, his own system of government, and his own laws. He believes this to be his God given right. The Muslim, on the other hand, believes that his destiny is unalterable, his system of government has been established, by the Qur'an and the Sunnah, and that law can come only from the law givers (i.e. Allah and His Prophet. (saw).

Desiring of the Muslim, that he abandon the notion that what Allah revealed, in the Qur'an is the absolute truth, and is to ask him to become a Muslim, in name only. He is effectively being asked to take parts of the book, believe in it, and take other parts and then disbelieve in them. He is, with certainty, being asked to declare that his God is a Liar! There are, without question, Muslims who are willing to declare that democracy is superior to the laws of Allah (swt). There have and always will be people willing to sell the next life for this one. However, when we find such Muslims, making such declarations we can state with absolute certainty that they are not representing Islam as revealed in the Quran, nor do they support the position of the Prophet of Islam.

One would have to struggle mightily to move his tongue, to say that he believes that the Qur'an is the unaltered word of God, sent as guidance to mankind, through the Prophet Muhammad (saw), yet still at the same time claiming that he believes that it is lawful, according to Qur'an, for the Muslim to willingly accept and or embrace a system of government other than the rule of law, as reveled by Allah (swt).

The difficulty such a one would face is that he would have to make such claims in defiance to what Allah (swt) (whom he holds to be God) revealed, in the Qur'an. There are six successive ayaat (verses), in the Qur'an, which established the textual basis, for Islamic Shari'ah being the only system of government acceptable to the Muslims. In the following six verses, we read what means:

> "Indeed, We sent down the Torah, in which was guidance and light. The Prophets who submitted (to Allah) judge by it for the Jews, as did the Rabbis and scholars by that with which they were entrusted or the Scripture of Allah, and they were witnesses thereto. So do not fear the people but fear Me and do not

exchange My verses for a small price (i.e. worldly gain). And whoever does not judge by what Allah has revealed then it is those who are the disbelievers."

"We ordained therein for them an eye for an eye, nose for nose, tooth for tooth and wounds equal for equal. But if any one remits the retaliation, by way of charity, it is an act of atonement for himself. And if any fails to judge (rule) by what Allah revealed, they are wrongdoers."

"And, in their footsteps, We sent Jesus the son of Mary, confirming the Torah that had come before him: We sent him the Gospel: therein was guidance and light. And confirmation, of the Toraha that had come before him. A guidance and an admonition, for those who fear Allah."

"Let,the people, of the Gospel judge (rule) by what Allah hath revealed therein. If any do fail to judge by what Allah hath revealed, they are those who rebel."

"And We have revealed to you (0 Muhammad), the Book (i.e. The qur'an) in truth, confirming that which preceded it of scripture and as a criterion over it. So judge between them by what Allah has revealed and do not follow their inclination way from what has come to you of the truth. To each of you We have prescribed a law and a method. Had Allah willed He would have made you one nation, but (He intended) to test you in what He has given you: so race to good. To Allah is your return altogether, and He will inform you concerning that over which you used to differ."

"And this (He commands): judge (rule) thou between them by what Allah has revealed. And follow not their vain desires, but beware of them lest they beguile thee from any of that of the (teachings) which Allah hath sent down to thee. And if they turn away, be assured that for some of their crimes it is Allah's purpose to punish them. And truly most men are rebellious."

The six preceding ayaat (verses) are most instructive, in this matter, we find here that the Qur'an is instructing the Prophet Muhammad, the example to all Muslims, that he, even he must judge by what Allah has revealed in the Qur'an and what Allah (swt) has revealed directly to him for the purpose of establishing the correct example. Now this may not be immediately clear to a person reading the text, but examination reveals this to be true.

When we look to the first verse (44) what we find is that Allah (swt) is speaking to the Prophet Muhammad (saw) explaining to him (saw) that He, Allah (swt), had previously revealed to Musa

A.S. (Moses) the Torah and that it was a book of guidance during his life time and after. Allah explains that the Torah was entrusted to the Jews, the Rabbis and the Doctors of law for protection. It was the book of guidance and light. Then Allah (swt) stops explaining to the Prophet Muhammad (saw) about the history of the Torah and issues him a command and it is:

"Fear not men, but fear Me!"

And then Allah (swt) goes further to say what means:

"And sell not my ayaat (signs, verses) for a miserable price.

Then He (swt) says what means:

"If any do fail to judge by what Allah has revealed they are disbelievers."

Allah (swt) was making clear to the Prophet (saw) and his followers, which the duty was to judge, by the Qur'an, as it had been the duty of Musa A.S. (Moses) and his followers to judge, by the Torah. Allah established that failing to do so made this failure an act of disbelief. In ayah (verse) 45, Allah (swt) tells us that as a matter, of Torahic, law that it was an eye for an eye, but that as a matter of the law now, i.e. Qur'anic law, there is a provision that leaving off retaliation will be, for the remitter, a means by which he can atone for some of his own sins. Then Allah (swt) again issues the admonition that judging by anything other than the current revelation (i.e. Qur'an) is an act which cause one to become a wrong-doer.

The next verse (46) serves to reaffirm that books of revelation from Allah (swt) to His Prophets, are books of guidance and light, meaning they must be followed, and that therein is not only guidance but admonition. The likes of which we find each time Allah (swt) speaks about failing to judge by what He (swt) revealed.

In verse (47) we fired that Allah (swt) says what means:

> "Let the people of the Gospel, judge, by what Allah hath revealed therein. If any do fail to judge by what Allah revealed they are those who rebel"

We note that Allah (swt) did not command the Prophet (saw) to judge the People of the Gospel according to the Gospel, but that the people of the Gospel should themselves use the Gospel as guidance and light and that judging, by something other than what Allah had revealed was open rebellion.

Verse (48), is the most revealing, with respect to our current discussion. It is in this verse, that we find the language that clarifies the need, for the Muslim, to reject any system of judging, ruling which is not based on the laws of Allah (swt) as revealed, by Allah (swt), either, in Qur'an or the Sunnah of His (saw) Prophet (saw). The portion of the verse that says "... and as a criterion over it. "makes clear that the Qur'an is a criterion over all the previously mentioned scriptures. The actual Arabic word used is "Muhaimin" which means "Superseding". Allah begins the verse by asserting that the Prophet Muhammad (saw) was recipient to the same as was the Prophets that Allah (swt) had just mentioned (i.e. Musa A.S. (Moses) and 'Isa A.S. (Jesus) (peace be upon both of them). Allah makes clear that the current book (scripture) is a confirmation of what was revealed before it. This is important because Allah (swt), in the previous verses, makes mention of previous books (scriptures), yet still commands His Messenger to use only the current book (i.e. Qur'an) to judge with. In this verse, this becomes clear when we read the wording:

> "So judge between them by what Allah hath revealed
> and follow not their vain desires, diverging from the
> truth that hath come to thee..."

If one is tempted to understand these six verses to mean that the Prophet Muhammad (saw) was commanded to judge the Jews and Christians, in accordance with their own book, the following will, Inshallah, disabuse such a one, of that notion. We read what means:

"... and follow not their vain desires, diverging from the truth, which hath come to thee..."

This is clearly a reference the Qur'an, for that is the only book that had been sent to the Prophet Muhammad (saw). We will remember, from previous chapters, in this text, that the Prophet Muhammad (saw), undertook a non-aggression pact with all the people of Madinah, that pact was part and parcel, of a larger agreement. That larger agreement included a provision wherein all the people of Madinah agreed that the Prophet Muhammad (saw) would serve as the city's chief abator, it is for this reason, that we find these six verses, in the Qur'an. The Prophet (saw) had occasion, to judge, in a very real sense, the actions of both Jews and Christians. In that capacity his (saw) judgment was not according to the Torah or the Gospel, but the Qur'an, even though both the Torah and the Gospel were revealed by Allah.

It is clear that the Qur'an's place, in the pantheon of revealed books was to be the final word. For the next thing which Allah (swt) says is what means:

"... to each among you have We prescribed a law (Shir'ah) and on open way (Minhaj)..."

The prescriptions are here delineated. Each had been prescribed a separate Shir'ah and Minhaj. One will note the similarity between

110

the word Shir'ah and Shari'ah that is because they are derived from the some root and have ostensibly, the same meaning. So we find that the Qur'an says that each of these groups Jews, Christians, and later the Muslims was given its own law. Not only were they given their own law to follow, by also what has been translated as an "open way". The Arabic term is "Minhaj" and is better translated as a methodology.

A methodology is a way or means by which to accomplish a goal, it is, by definition a pattern of conduct and a repeatable phenomenon. The Shir'ah or law is clearly what Allah repeatedly refers to as what He (swt) revealed, the Minhaj is therefore none other than the Sunnah of various prophets mentioned, in these six verses. For the Sunnah (or the way) of the Prophets, is the pattern of conduct it is the means by which one can reach the proper application, of the Shir'ah (law). The Sunnah of these Prophets can be followed, that is to say, repeated.

So if each was sent their own law, and their own methodology, and the Qur'an commands the Prophet to judge, by the Shir'ah that was sent to him, by the Minhaj that he had established with Allah's guidance, how do we come to a place in time where we believe it fit or proper for one who calls himself Muslim and claims to be an adherent to the religion of Islam, to also claim that

111

any system of governance other than the Sharia'ah is acceptable to those who adhere to the Qur'an.

Verse (49) is the nail that seals the coffin. In it, Allah reiterates to the Prophet (saw) the command to judge, by the Qur'an, and to be wary of judging, by anything but the Qur'an. This is because as the revelation that came last, it was the revelation which Allah chose to supersede all previous revelation. This is known owing to the fact that the Prophet(saw) was commanded to give deference to the Qur'an, in judgment, over that of the Torah and the Gospel.

As we have noted before, there are those Muslims who will say that democracy is better than Islamic Shari'ah, or perhaps they say that there is no conflict between Islam and democracy. We can no doubt find countless Muslims who will tell you that a Muslim can be a loyal citizen of a democratic nation or any nation other than one which has established the Shari'ah. The reality, however, is that all such Muslims will find it difficult beyond all difficulties to produce, from the Qur'an, any proof to establish that claim.

It may be that there is difficulty in hearing the truth, but the truth defeats all falsehood. The truth of the matter is that a Muslim who is truly following the Qur'an, is always seeking to establish the law of Allah (swt), first in his own life and then in the society at large. That is the Minhaj (methodology) of the Prophet of Islam Muhammad ibn Abdullah (saw).

Now that it is known that Islam is principally at odds with western style democracies, and all other systems of governance, for that matter, what are the implications of this knowledge?

We have sought exhaustively to establish that Islam is a religion of peace, and here we too have established that Islam is in conflict with every other system of government. Why, it may be asked, cannot this religion of peace find a way to reconcile itself with the rest of the world? The answer is simple. To do so would require Islam to disappear, to become nothing more than a cult of ritual worshipers having no real belief, disregarding the foundation of Islam itself.

That notwithstanding, Islam can and has always peacefully co-existed with people with whom they disagree. What the Muslim cannot abide, as a matter of law, are a people who actively seek to destroy Islam, in its true form, replacing it with a watered down version, useful only to Allah's enemies. Nor can the Muslims abide a peaceful coexistence with a people who aid and support the killing of Muslims, the expelling of Muslims from their homes, or the denial of Muslims, the right to establish the Shari'ah. This in effect means that if Islam is to enjoy peaceful relations with the west and western style democracy, then the west will necessarily have to abandon their quest to democratize the so called middle-east and other Muslim lands.

It is perhaps shocking to some that one can say that Islam desires peace, desires non-aggression, desires normalized relations with the other nations, of the world but this is in fact true. This, however, does not mean that Islam desires these things to the detriment of its own existence. Given a choice between peaceful co-existence with nations that neither recognize nor respect the rights of Muslim nations to establish and rule by the law of Allah, and hostilities, then Islam chooses hostilities. The alternative is to agree with these nations, agree that Islam, as practiced by the Prophet Muhammad (saw), as revealed, by Allah (swt), in the Qur'an, has no place in the modern world and must be transformed and stripped of its principals; that the Muslims have no right, nor obligation to fight, when necessary, to make the word of Allah (swt) supreme.

Certainly can pass over everyone who has occasion to contemplate this matter, as long as there is a Qur'an, on this earth, there will be Muslims who seek to follow it. As long as there are Muslims who seek to follow the Qur'an, there will be Muslims who believe that it is the word of Allah, (swt), binding on all Muslims, who believe in Allah (swt) and the Last Day. One may speak with truth and certainty, should he say that as long as such Muslims breathe breath, that some of them will resist, with force if necessary, individuals and even nations, who seek to stomp out Islam and its proper practice.

It therefore appears to be most simple to comprehend the reality with which the world is currently faced. If the so called International community, headed by the United States, is unwilling to sit by idly and witness that rise of an Islamic nation that rules solely and truly, by the Shari'ah, a nation which is beholden not to the U.N. or its member states, but is guided by what is and is not permissible accord1ng to Islam, then conflict is inevitable. This conflict however, is not, nor will it be a result of Muslim or Islamic aggression, but rather the unwillingness on the part of the so called international community, to allow for Muslim self-determination. This is owning to the fact, that there are those from amongst the Muslim populace who understands and accepts that they have a duty to Allah (swt) to establish such a nation, ruled by Shari'ah.

It is hoped that the Muslim who finds it necessary, according to their faith, to resist the forceful winds of change, do so while giving full faith and credit to both the limits of war set by Allah (swt) and His Messenger (saw), we pray that those who fight, in the cause of Allah are heedful, of the Book, for which they claim to fight. We leave those who seek Islam as their faith, Jihaad as their obligation, Muhammad (saw) as their Messenger (saw) and Allah (swt) as their God, with what follows:

> "Fight, in the cause, of Allah, those who fight you, but do not transgress the bounds, for Allah loves not those who transgress." Qur'an 2:190

> "0 you who believe! Stand out firmly, for Allah as witnesses to fair dealing, and LET NOT YOUR HATRED FOR A PEOPLE make you swerve from justice. Be just. That is next to piety and fear Allah. For Allah is well acquainted with all that you do." Qur'an 5:8

CONCLUSION

People who, for whatever reason, don't believe in Islam as the only true religion, in the sight of God, have at a minimum some philosophical or spiritual variance with what Muslims believe. None should find this strange, for this is the case with every religion known to man. If we collectively believed the same, we would all be the same. These differences, however, don't need to be a cause for conflict, hatred, and the like. Muslims are perfectly content to develop and maintain peaceful relations, with people who do not fight us for our faith.

What needs to be understood and respected is that it is the Muslim who decides what is and is not a part of the faith, and this decision results from a methodology that does not permit outside influences or suggestions. Islam is a religion which is unalterable at its core. Should that be accepted, by non-Muslims, they would then be free to decide if they wish to interact with the Muslims. Should they decide to interact with the Muslims, we would hope that this interaction would be on the basis of recognition and respect for Islamic principles. If the decision is taken that Islam is so fundamentally different, as to make the Muslim strangers that they do not wish to interact with, that too is welcome by the Muslim.

If such a balance was struck, then at least some of the rationale used by the so-called Muslim terrorist, would disappear. These animals who slaughter children, in the name of the Most Loving God, are enemies to all God fearing people. They threaten Islam more than they threaten its enemies, but there is great difficulty in seeking to rationalize the prohibition of the conflict itself. The means by which this conflict is being conducted is clearly condemned by Allah (swt) and His Messenger (saw). Just as, in the hadeeth, wherein Ali (RA) was reported to have burned the apostates. He had a right to put them to death, yet the method was condemned, by Allah (swt) and His Messenger (saw), and when his conduct became known to Ibn Abbas (Ra) he too condemned the modality, but not the underlying act itself.

If one was to be completely fair when viewing this matter of so-called Islamic terrorism, one would be forced to concede that targeting civilian populations as a means of war, may be a tactic of other nations, but that the tactic is rejected by Islam. Unfortunately, we live in a time in which when something is rejected by Islam, it doesn't necessarily follow that it is rejected by the Muslims. This is an abomination of the highest order. The Muslim should be a reflection of Islam and not his passions. So when we find a relative few number of Muslims, defaming the religion and behaving, in ways, that neither the Qur'an nor the

Sunnah can abide, we have to know that even if they represented every Muslim on the planet, which they most certainly do not, they would still be acting outside of the dictates of Islam, they would still be sinning against their souls. Such people would undoubtedly be earning the wrath of Allah, The Most Compassionate, The Most Merciful.

If one does not seek to be fair, then he should be ignored. He is of little intellect and no character. The Muslim and non-Muslim alike would be better served by laying on the table the facts as they exist, argue from a position of truth, and let the recrimination fall where they may.

The Muslim will expend his energies in seeking to explain what Islam is, and what it is not, we will speak to what Islam permits and what it prohibits. What the Muslim must never do, should never do is apologize, in any way, for this wonderful, amazing, dynamic and peace loving religion. Islam is what Islam is. One is free to except or reject that, but the man of mind and intellect cannot, having read what came before, maintain that Islam invites to what, for the lack of a better term has been named ISLAMIC TERRORISM.

....

May 30, 2006
Susanville
California USA

www.ingramcontent.com/pod-product-compliance
Lightning Source LLC
Chambersburg PA
CBHW060941040426
42445CB00011B/955